– THE –
BRILLIANT
MANIPULATOR

– THE –
BRILLIANT
MANIPULATOR

ritu arora

Notion Press

Old No. 38, New No. 6
McNichols Road, Chetpet
Chennai - 600 031

First Published by Notion Press 2017
Copyright © Ritu Arora 2017
All Rights Reserved.

ISBN 978-1-947137-80-6

Contents

Foreword

After a pretty long time, I got a draft book authored by Ritu Arora for my perusal and to write a FOREWORD.

Reading the book was a great experience. Ritu Arora being an experienced banker picked up a transaction from Treasury Operations of a Bank to structure the entire episode involving fraud. The whole story moves around the fraud to portray intractable human nature/behaviour.

Multiple thoughts always generate in the mind of a human being; some of them are positive and many of them are negative heading towards disaster. We sometimes wonder as to why someone behaves or acts in a particular way. Sometimes a person acts inappropriately which could be with or without any motive/intention. The narration in the book is in conversational format that keeps the suspense and interest alive in the mind of a reader.

I recommend this book to be read by everybody in general and the professional banker in particular as the technical transaction has been narrated in the most simple language.

P M Pethe

Forex Consultant & Trainer

OSD-Training, FEDAI

Mumbai

Preface

Interacting with people is a part of our daily routine. Be it at the workplace, place of study, playground or social gatherings, we meet people of different beliefs, values, skills, intellect and ages; this makes life vibrant and interesting.

My career as a banker introduced me to various kinds of personalities. But I dare not classify them as good or bad, patient or impatient, honest or dishonest, because I don't want to be judgmental. Seeing the good in every person is my new mantra for life.

As a banker, one experiences and witnesses incidents of financial fraud when a gullible soul succumbs to temptation. On some occasions, seemingly minor incidents throw the otherwise mundane life of a banker out of gear, into the ocean of uncertainties.

I have always marveled at people who are creative. I have always admired artists, designers, authors, poets, sculptors, actors, singers, dancers, musicians and scientists and thought they were a class apart. But I never envied them as I was convinced that god had made me so ordinary that I was unique in my own way.

It was a chance meeting with a scriptwriter during a train journey from Mumbai to New Delhi in April, 2015 that made me pen this book. His words "you can weave stories from your experience with people and a little imagination" remained with me long after the journey ended. A thought ignited in my mind. *Why do brilliant minds commit crime? What goes behind their thought process? What makes them break the rules?*

As the saying goes, "No risk, no profit and higher the risk, higher the profit." A posting in the Treasury department of a bank is the most coveted position for a banker. Only the most brilliant people are chosen to deal with huge amounts of money and are encouraged to take risks and book profits. But as a brilliant mind gains experience, the thin line that divides risk-taking and flouting the rules becomes blurry and the mind starts justifying every wrong action as a tool of risk. This book is a story of one such brilliant mind who flouted rules and how the fraud that emerged from this put many of his colleagues under the scanner. Will the Brilliant Manipulator get away with this fraud?

Acknowledgments

My heartfelt thanks to my friends, Rama Kannan, Shirley Katyal and Kishore Rao Naimpally for their patience in evaluating the draft manuscript, encouragement and valuable suggestions.

My special thanks to Mr. Steven D Levitt, Professor of Economics at the University of Chicago, for very kindly permitting me to quote his article 'Many parallels between trading in financial markets and sports betting'.

Sketch Artist Ameya Benare

1

The Treasury Branch

It was the winter of 2011 on the 27th day of December. As the international markets were readying for the Christmas and New Year holidays, it was business as usual in the financial markets of Delhi. While the winds outside were depressingly cold, the air-conditioners in the dealing room of ZNI Bank's Treasury department, along with the heat of the frenetic activities, maintained the temperature at comfortable levels.

The last week of the quarter was crucial for completing the business targets. The forex markets were choppy and the corporates were nervous. With the rupee getting weaker in the last few weeks, exporters had been holding on to their dollar reserves, while the importers waited anxiously hoping for an improvement in the European debt crisis or the central bank's intervention.

The dealing room of ZNI Bank reflected the uncertainty outside. A dozen-odd dealers were glued to their screens. Only Anand Patel and Deepak Pandit were on their mandatory annual leave.

As merchant dealer Lalit Jain snapped the ringing of the incoming call, it was Adorn Exports Ltd (AEL) at the other end.

"Quote for $20 mio. (million), I sell."

"51.94."

"What after 94?"

"Nothing."

"Come on, give me the third and fourth decimals."

"Obviously 00."

"Who is on the line?"

"Lalit."

"Where is Anand?"

"On leave, why do you ask?"

The line went dead. AEL had chosen to hang up.

Lalit was pondering over the conversation for a few seconds when the phone rang again. It was another client.

"Quote for $5 mio, I buy."

The excitement, noise and hustle-bustle continued throughout the day. The top boss at the Treasury department, Amit Tandon, was seen moving around, shooting orders, speaking over the phone, reporting to his superiors, and making notes on the small writing pad he always carried around.

The Treasury department of ZNI Bank was located on the twelfth floor of the twenty-storied Empire Tower in the upmarket Connaught Place, New Delhi. It was one of the few sophisticated treasuries among the banks in India, with state-of-the-art technology.

The dictionary defines 'Treasury' as a place where the treasure is stored. In the olden days, this is where the treasures of the rulers were stored. In modern times, Treasury is the place where the funds of a government/corporation /organization are routed for receipts and disbursements. In a bank, the Treasury is the division or branch where funds and cash flows are managed on a day-to-day basis and liquidity is recycled to maximize returns within acceptable risk levels, based on the parameters stipulated by the central bank of the country.

Banks have come a long way from being mere institutions that accepted deposits and lent money to being major participants in the financial markets. As borders between countries opened for trade and more and more people started traveling across the world, there arose a need for trading foreign currencies. Due to liberalization and deregulation of economies by many countries, the entire world has become one big market. The advent of sophisticated financial instruments and products over the years, coupled with an increase in the number of financial players, has made the financial market highly competitive and prone to risk.

Over a period of time, managing the liquidity of a bank's surplus funds and its deployment across domestic and global forex markets to maximize profits and enhance shareholder value became a specialized job. This job was later delegated to a specialized division of the bank called the Treasury branch, with two verticals, namely local trade (domestic treasury) and foreign trade (forex treasury). The job of managing funds in the local currency is assigned to the domestic treasury. Managing cross-border trade across multiple currencies, maintaining accounts with overseas correspondent banks (Nostro accounts) in major foreign currencies, tracking the inflow and outflow from these accounts, matching all debit and credit entries and the balances therein, within the guidelines laid down by the regulator as well as the counterpart country, and making these transactions profitable come under the domain of the forex treasury.

2

The Dealer

Like all banks, the Treasury branch of ZNI Bank was bifurcated into domestic and forex treasury, each with its own front and back offices. The front office is like a marketplace where banks sit with their products and buyers and sellers trade with them, the only difference being the business is transacted electronically. The traders of the bank are called dealers.

In the forex treasury, the front office is the main center of activity with monitors flashing live data from across continents, phones and hot lines ringing constantly, and huge television screens displaying the latest news.

The job of a dealer entails giving quotes for sale and purchase of foreign currency to clients, covering open positions, and trading to make profits. The sharpest and brightest young men and women, who are willing to take risks, are chosen for the coveted post of a dealer. Those with a quick analytical mind, who regularly track the happenings around the world that impact the forex market, are able to deliver the desired results. But the pressure of failure is enormous. So is the probability of acquiring a mightier-than-thou attitude on continuous delivery of positive results. The mere mention of being a forex dealer draws admiring looks and jaw-dropping awe from colleagues. No wonder that most dealers appear to inhabit a world isolated from the others, in the midst of screens, phones and monitors.

Very close to the dealing room is the forex back office, which houses the staff who keep an eye on the quotes given by the dealers in line with the market, coordinate between the bank's branches and the dealing room, maintain a record of the deals of the day, and match all the incoming and outgoing rupee and foreign currency flow. Though the pressure is lesser in this department, there is a critical need to maintain accuracy and alertness at all times.

The mid office is a vital section of the Treasury; it keeps a hawk eye on the operations of the dealing room, in line with the policies and guidelines of the bank and the directives of the central bank of the country. Maintaining compliance is a key responsibility of this office; any deviations are promptly reported to the higher authorities for corrective action.

The forex treasury department of ZNI Bank had seven dealers in the dealing room, six officers in the back office, and four in the mid office. All the offices were housed on the same sprawling floor.

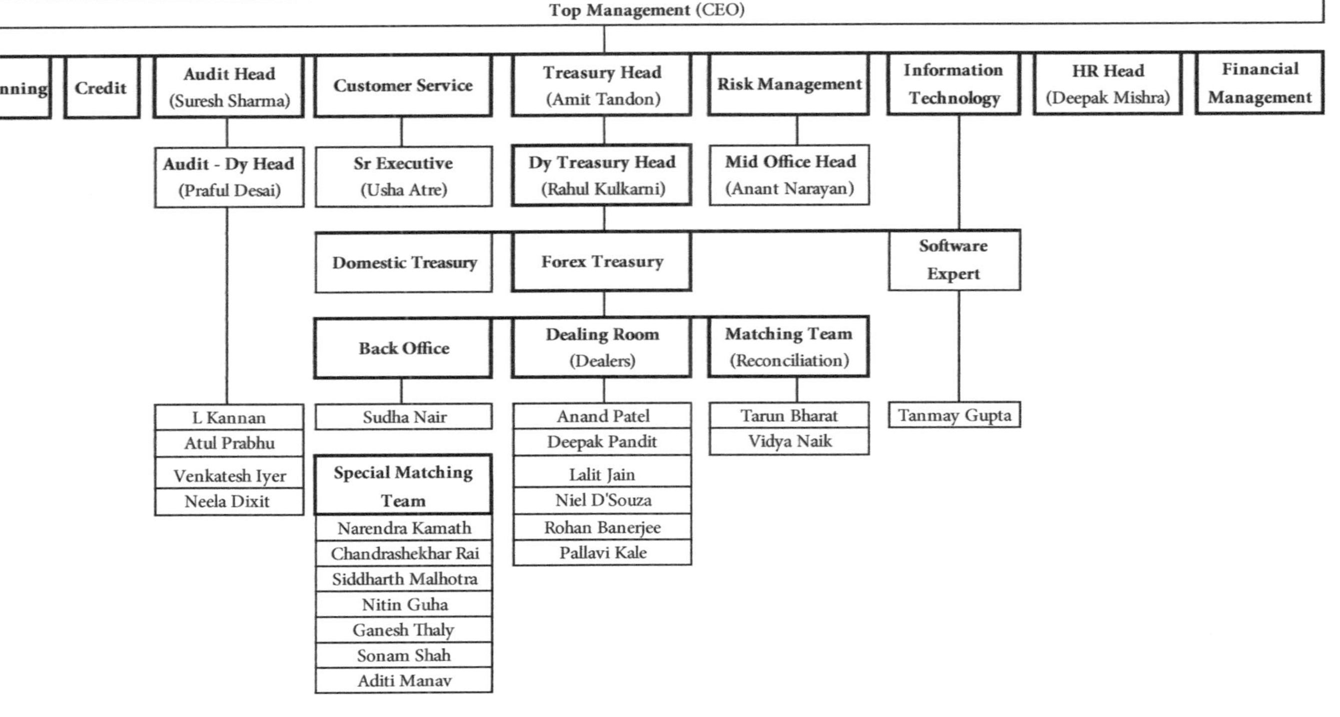

Top Management (CEO)
Planning
Credit
Audit Head (Suresh Sharma)
Customer Service
Treasury Head (Amit Tandon)
Risk Management
Information Technology
HR Head (Deepak Mishra)
Financial Management
Audit - Dy Head (Praful Desai)
Sr Executive (Usha Atre)
Dy Treasury Head (Rahul Kulkarni)
Mid Office Head (Anant Narayan)
Domestic Treasury
Forex Treasury
Software Expert
Back Office
Dealing Room (Dealers)
Matching Team (Reconciliation)
L Kannan
Atul Prabhu
Venkatesh Iyer
Neela Dixit
Sudha Nair
Special Matching Team
Narendra Kamath
Chandrashekhar Rai
Siddharth Malhotra
Nitin Guha
Ganesh Thaly
Sonam Shah
Aditi Manav
Anand Patel
Deepak Pandit
Lalit Jain
Niel D'Souza
Rohan Banerjee
Pallavi Kale
Tarun Bharat
Vidya Naik
Tanmay Gupta

3

The Mystery

Lalit Jain

On the evening of December 27, 2011, the dealers, after reporting the day's transactions, closing positions and resultant profit/loss, were on their way out. Reaching home, catching up on sleep to be able to return fresh the next morning, with relevant study of the markets that were now operating in the other end of the world, was their next goal.

Lalit boarded the metro train to return to his house in Karol Bagh. Though he could afford a chauffeur-driven car, he preferred to travel by the metro to save time and avoid the slow-moving traffic. On his way home, he would often get into a flashback mode and rewind the day's happening in his mind. It was his way of learning from his mistakes. Today, his mind went back to the conversation with AEL.

"Quote for $20 mio (million). I sell."

"51.94."

"What after 94?"

"Nothing."

"Come on, give me the third and fourth decimals."

"Obviously 00."

"Who is on the line?"

"Lalit."

"Where is Anand?"

"On leave, why do you ask?"

And then there was deafening silence as the line went dead.

Lalit pondered over the third and fourth decimals. The rates were always quoted in two decimals, except for a couple of clients who had very large transactions (this was done with special sanctions from the higher authorities). Then why did the caller ask what after 94, wondered Lalit. His thoughts were interrupted by an argument between a few commuters—a common feature during the peak hours.

Now, Lalit's thoughts were diverted towards the complexity of human nature. He lamented the fact that absence or scarcity of resources brought out the animal traits in a human being. When human necessities were adequately met, people were generally patient, kind and well-mannered, but the slightest hint of scarcity brought out the survival instincts in them.

The train announced the arrival of his station and Lalit walked out of the train along with the other passengers.

The next few days were more hectic than the previous day. Lalit had no time to decipher the mystery of the third and fourth decimals query by AEL.

4

The Loss

Luckily for the Treasury department, the December quarter had ended with fairly good results. It was the first week of the new year and the bosses were relaxed and this percolated to the subordinates as well. A happy atmosphere prevailed in the office. However, Lalit Jain was disturbed. The dialogue about the third and fourth decimals kept playing in his mind. Finally, he decided to check the records.

Before leaving office in the evening, Lalit generated a report of the rates given to AEL from October to December, 2011. Nothing appeared amiss. All the rates had two decimal places. Lalit studied the report for about half an hour, after which he packed up and left office. But he could not sleep that night. The rate report kept flashing before his eyes. He cursed himself for not being able to control his mind.

The next morning, Lalit was unable to wake up on time and had to rush to work. That evening, he once again generated the rate report from October. Again, everything appeared normal. But, just as he was about to discard the report, an intuitive impulse made him pull out the calculator from the drawer. As he multiplied the dollar amount ($2,000,000) with the rate (51.53) to check the resultant rupee amount, he cursed himself for being silly and cross-checking computerized calculations. Obviously, the system could not make a mistake in multiplying. However, since he had already pulled out the calculator, Lalit thought he may as well compare.

$$(\$) \, 2,000,000 \times 51.53 = (Rs)103,060,000$$

But the rate report showed ($) 2,000,000 x 51.53 = (Rs) 103,073,000

Lalit wondered if he had made a mistake in punching the numbers on the calculator. He recalculated and got the same result. There was a difference of Rs 13,000. This cue made him check all the entries in the report. Every transaction had a difference in the rupee value, varying from 5,000 to 10,000 per million dollars. Intrigued, Lalit generated the rate report for other clients but found no such discrepancy. As he kept studying the reports, he did not realize that it was well past his usual winding-up time. Concerned and curious, his colleagues started enquiring about it. So, Lalit felt compelled to pack up and leave. Finally, the mystery of the third and fourth decimals seemed to make sense to Lalit. He would have to decide upon the next course of action.

The next morning, Lalit reached office half an hour earlier than usual and checked the rate report for the two valued clients who were sanctioned rate quotation in four decimal places. There too, the rate appeared in two decimal places and the rupee amount was higher than the product of the dollar and the rate. Lalit was aware that, for these two clients, the rates were manually corrected to four decimal places in the hard copies, which were then duly signed by the higher authorities. However, there was no such correction in the hard copies of AEL.

That Saturday, Lalit made an estimate of the turnover in the AEL account. It was approximately $400 million, which worked out to a gain of over twenty lakhs rupees per annum to AEL and a resultant loss to the bank, due to the third and fourth decimal quotes.

5

The Suspect

Anand Patel

Anand Patel was a dealer in his late twenties, like Lalit. Belonging to a fairly well-to-do family, he was blessed with many luxuries. Lalit was puzzled as to what could be Anand's reason for favoring a client. He wondered if there were more such clients whom he favored. After all, tens of lakhs of rupees per annum was not a small amount. Was Anand planning to move on to some other organization? Good dealers were always in demand in a competitive market. Anand was to rejoin duty on January 13, 2012. Lalit had a few days to decide and act accordingly. Should he just keep quiet or should he tell the boss? Would the boss take the disclosure in the right spirit? What if the boss was also involved in it? *No, Amit Tandon is an honest person, or at least appears so,* thought Lalit. But keeping quiet after stumbling upon the deceit would tantamount to being a party to it. *Damn middle-class morality,* thought Lalit.

As expected, Lalit could not sleep a wink that night. Numerous thoughts flitted through his mind. *Will Amit Tandon support me? After all, being the head of the Treasury department, he is answerable to his superiors. What about the auditors? Did they not notice anything amiss? Forget the auditors, what about the mid office? Why did they not notice this? Disclosing this would result in a lot of heads rolling. What should I do? Whom do I consult? Obviously, I too may have to face a lot of hassles in the ensuing inquiry,* thought Lalit.

If Anand lost his job, many would blame the one who opened the Pandora's box. After all, Anand was a much-admired colleague. He was young, handsome and always well-dressed, with a polished way of speaking. He could easily win over people with his looks, knowledge and conduct. Lalit was in a dilemma.

The next morning, Lalit called up his boss to inform him that he was unwell and could not attend office. The boss was kind enough to grant him a day's leave. But, as luck would have it, Lalit got an urgent call at noon from the office requesting him to come over as an urgent PowerPoint presentation had to be made. His help was required to collate the data. At first, Lalit was tempted to refuse. On second thoughts, he felt this was an opportunity to spend some time with Amit and gauge him. He reached office after lunch and got down to gathering the relevant data. He was compelled to stay back late to add the final touches to the presentation. Amit, who was sitting next to Lalit in the mini conference hall, had removed his tie and unbuttoned his shirt collar.

Amit Tandon

Amit was in his early forties, tall, big-built with a deep resonating voice. He had a chubby face and traces of gray in his thick mop of hair. Though he was huge in size, he had a benevolent disposition, which made people feel at ease with him.

Amit appeared like an elder brother to Lalit and he involuntarily blurted out the truth.

"Sir, I have something to share with you."

"Sure, go ahead, Lalit."

"Sir, not now, maybe later. Let's finish the presentation first."

"Well, I thought you were talking about the presentation."

"No sir, anyway it's not important."

Amit shrugged his shoulders and went on with his work. *Me and my big mouth,* thought Lalit. After finalizing the presentation, Lalit started packing up. Amit returned to his cabin and called for him.

"Lalit, now tell me what is it that you wanted to tell me."

"Sir, nothing. It is something silly."

"Lalit, I have been watching you over the last week. Tell me, what is it?"

Lalit's heart skipped a beat. He wondered if his predicament was so obvious. Was Amit a party to the fraud and had already been alerted by AEL?

"Lalit, you look disturbed. What's the matter? Any blunder you wish to confide?" pursued Amit.

"No, sir. Nothing to do with me."

"Then who?"

Again, Lalit wondered if Amit was aware of the whole thing and was just trying to get it out of him. Before he could come to a conclusion, Amit repeated, "Then who?"

"It's about Anand, sir."

Lalit then went on to report all that had happened. Throughout the narration, he kept keenly observing Amit's expressions, trying to gauge whether he too was a party to it. Amit's face was blank.

"Lalit, tomorrow I have to attend an important meeting. I shall ponder over what you have said after the meeting. Till then don't discuss this with anyone."

"Yes sir," said Lalit and left.

On his way back home, Lalit could not make up his mind as to whether he had done the right thing in disclosing the irregularity. But he was relieved that it was off his chest.

Contrary to Lalit's expectations, the next day turned out to be a pretty mundane one. Amit was away at the meeting for most part of the day. Just as Lalit and the others were winding up for the day, Amit returned from the meeting. He entered the dealing room smiling. He then announced loudly that the meeting was a grand success. He thanked Lalit profusely for making the presentation. After having a general discussion with the dealers about the day's business, Amit walked out of the dealing room asking Lalit to meet him in his cabin for a discussion on the day's meeting.

Lalit stiffened a bit. He was sure that this had nothing to do with the meeting. His instinct was to walk away home, but he decided against it. As he entered Amit's cabin, he noticed the PowerPoint presentation running on the computer. A hard copy of the presentation was thrown on the table. It was obvious that Amit wanted anyone walking into his cabin to think that the meeting was being discussed.

"Lalit, take a seat. Please repeat what you told me yesterday."

Amit coming straight to the previous day's discussion startled Lalit a bit. But there was no option but to go over it again. He narrated the conversation he had had with AEL and his observations thereof, without any interruption from Amit. It became obvious to Lalit that Amit had already pondered over the previous day's conversation as he asked relevant questions after Lalit finished. It was well-known to everyone that Amit had a very sharp mind. No wonder that he headed such a coveted department.

Closing his eyes, Amit contemplated for a few minutes. Then he summarized his thoughts into words.

"First of all, the rate reports were programmed to display rates in two decimal places, as the rates were always given in two decimal places only. It was later decided to quote rates in four decimal places for very valued clients only, that too for deals above $100 million.

Number two, the relevant changes to print four-digit decimal rates were not incorporated in the software; the requirement somehow was overlooked.

Three, but for that day's slip on the part of AEL staff, coupled with your curiosity and perseverance, Anand's favor to AEL would have continued.

Four, are there more clients being favored by Anand?

Five, are other dealers also favoring some clients?

And finally, obviously, the matter has to be probed further and the higher-ups have to be informed."

Lalit sat there, musing over Amit's clarity of thought. His admiration for the man increased manifold. Meanwhile, Amit called the onsite software staff and asked them to generate a rate report where clients were quoted rates in four decimal places. He impressed upon them that the data was required to be placed before the senior management.

The experienced software team generated the report immediately. It came as a big relief to both Amit and Lalit to see that AEL was the only client in the list other than the valued MNC clients (who were sanctioned the four-decimal privilege). Amit then asked the software team for an additional column of data with the dealers' names. Again, there was only one name—Anand Patel.

Amit thanked Lalit and asked him to go home, saying that he would take appropriate action.

Lalit left office and walked towards the metro station. He was surprised that he neither felt excited nor remorseful. Amit had ended the meeting so abruptly. Was Amit playing some game with him? Had he done the right thing in disclosing everything to him? Such thoughts continued to assail Lalit.

6

The Charge

On the 13th of January 2012, Anand was to resume duty. Around 8:30 a.m., the dealers started trickling into office. Anand came in, noisily greeting everyone and answering innumerable questions about his vacation. Just then, the office boy motioned to Anand that the big boss wanted to meet him. Anand confidently walked towards Amit's cabin.

Lalit had been observing Anand since his entry into the office. Seeing Anand being summoned, his heart beat increased. He eagerly awaited Anand's return to the dealing room. Half an hour later, Anand had still not returned. An hour went by. Then two and then three hours. Anand was still not back. Nobody seemed to miss Anand, as they were all busy with their work. It was around 2 o'clock in the afternoon when Lalit decided to check with Amit. "Anand got an urgent call from his hometown regarding his grandma's stroke. He will be back next week," said Amit.

Lalit returned to his seat wondering what was going on. As he passed by the audit room, he saw two officers from the audit department of the head office talking to a few staff members. The back office colleagues were seen walking in and out of the audit room, seemingly providing the officers some records.

A week passed by. Anand, who was on leave, was called to the office and given a letter. He was suspected of having committed the following irregularities and was asked to compulsorily remain on leave till further instructions.

a. Undue favor to M/s Adorn Exports Ltd.

b. Defrauding the bank to the tune of Rs 25 lakhs by sending $50,000 overseas, through the Interbank Global Messaging system, during the period September 2008-December 2009.

Heads started to roll. Anant Narayan, who was heading the mid office since 2007, was transferred to another city for failure to detect Anand Patel's fraud. Amit was lucky to be let off with a letter from his seniors deriding the lapse. The second irregularity had been committed before Amit had joined the Treasury, for which the earlier head was answerable.

Anand was shocked on seeing the charges. He refused to accept the letter.

"Boss, the first charge is correct. I am guilty of it. But I don't understand the second charge," said Anand.

"Systems don't lie," retorted Amit. "After the investigations are completed, the charges will be framed and you can file your say."

"Sir, can you at least tell me something about the second charge? I insist that I am not guilty of it," pleaded Anand.

Amit hesitated. He too had found it hard to believe Anand's involvement in the second charge. "Anand, the investigating team is preparing a detailed report, a copy of which will be made available to this office. You can access it then. And please keep all this confidential in your own interest."

Anand walked out of the office wondering what was in store for him. Favoring AEL had proved to be a big blunder. How had he even believed that it would go unnoticed? Initially, he had decided to do it for a few months. But immediate success and a sense of adventure proved too tempting to stop it.

But the second charge was absolutely false. Anand was baffled. What did it say? "Defrauding the bank to the tune of Rs 25 lakhs by sending $50,000 overseas through the Interbank Global Messaging system, during the period September 2008-December 2009." He read it again and then again, standing helplessly at the entrance of Empire Tower.

Anand Patel, twenty-eight years of age, a chartered accountant and an MBA from a prestigious institute, belonged to a well-to-do family. He lived in a flat owned by his parents in the posh Chanakyapuri area of New Delhi. His father ran a successful business in Surat, trading in chemicals. Money was not a problem for Anand nor was the prospect of landing a lucrative job. He could always join his father's business. Then, what was the reason for favoring AEL?

Anand did not want to ponder over his sudden predicament. Deep down, he knew his weakness for breaking the rule. Every time he saw a board that said 'no entry', he was tempted to enter it. It seemed as though his brain was programmed to defy restrictions. Though he managed to overcome this weakness most of the times, he could not crush it completely. Often this weakness got him into trouble. But today he had to pay a very heavy price for it. Would any sensible person believe that he did it on account of his weakness to break the rules?

But then, what about the second charge? "Defrauding the bank to the tune of Rs 25 lakhs by sending $50,000 overseas through the Interbank Global Messaging system, during the period September 2008-December 2009."

Anand read it and reread it. Something was terribly wrong. He ran towards his parked car, got into it and drove to the main office of the bank in Nehru Place. The drive from Connaught Place to Nehru Place that day seemed to be his longest drive ever. After crossing the hurdle of finding a parking slot, he hurried towards the elevator. As he entered the lift, he recognized a couple of colleagues. He avoided making any eye contact with them. They too did not seem to notice him. Anand wondered how far this news had spread.

The lift stopped on the 19th floor. Anand walked straight towards the cabin of Deepak Mishra, the chief of human resources (HR). Peering through the glass viewer on the door, he saw that Deepak was alone in his cabin. He knocked on the door and pushed it open.

"May I come in, sir?"

"Come in," came the prompt reply from Deepak.

"Sir, I am Anand Patel, forex dealer at Treasury. I have been sent on compulsory leave and I need to talk to you urgently."

Deepak was taken aback. He had heard about the case in the morning but he had not expected Anand to approach him directly. Being an honest man with a high sense of justice, Deepak could not refuse to talk to Anand. He took a few minutes to weigh the pros and cons of giving an audience to a suspended employee. Obviously, he would have to listen to Anand in his official capacity as the HR chief. *Would it be appropriate?* Deepak wondered. *Never mind, I shall look into that later,* decided Deepak.

"Okay Anand tell me. But you are probably aware that HR may not be able to do much at this stage."

"Sir, I am aware of that, but my purpose of meeting you is different," said Anand, as he placed the letter he had received before Deepak. "Sir, please read this communication to me. It accuses me of two wrongdoings. The first one I accept, but not the second. My sincere request to you is to ask the authorities to ensure that the second charge is not made public so that the actual culprit can be caught. If word about the second charge spreads, the actual culprit may try to destroy the records, which could otherwise prove my innocence. Sir, please."

Deepak pondered over the request. He then spoke into the intercom, requesting Suresh Sharma, the chief of the audit department, to come to his cabin. Deepak briefed Suresh about Anand and his request. "Suresh, I don't see any harm in acceding to Anand's request as he himself cannot access any records without permission," said Deepak.

"I agree, Deepak. The entire development has been kept highly confidential. I shall give instructions to have all records at Treasury under lock and key and ensure a register is maintained for any access to the records."

"Thank you, sir. I shall never forget your kindness," said Anand, as he prepared to leave.

"I hope my belief in you does not backfire," said Deepak.

As the door closed behind Anand, both Deepak and Suresh were silent. Anand's discomfiture had disturbed them. After a few minutes, Suresh confided to Deepak that as he had been abroad for a seminar and had returned only the previous night, he was not completely aware of the facts of the case. His secretary had mentioned the case briefly to him in the morning.

"Oh! Is that so?" exclaimed Deepak.

"Yes. But I shall immediately look into the case and get myself acquainted with all the facts," said Suresh.

"Do tell me in detail all the facts of this case after updating yourself, Suresh. Now that Anand has approached me, I am curious."

"Surely," assured Suresh as he left Deepak's cabin.

Suresh Sharma

Suresh Sharma reached his cabin and called the investigating team that comprised L. Kannan, Atul Prabhu, Venkatesh Iyer and Neela Dixit. He instructed them not to disclose anything to anyone. He then called them over to his office after lunch to get all the facts of the case.

Meanwhile, Anand left the main office trying to decide his course of action. He was aware that he would require a lot of cooperation from the staff at Treasury. He felt relieved that Deepak Mishra and Suresh Sharma had cooperated with him.

On reaching home, Anand debated whether to inform his parents or not about his compulsory leave. Then he decided not to put them on the path of worry. As he reached for his mobile, which he had put on silent mode while at the main office, he saw a number of missed calls from his parents. *Why so many calls?* he wondered. He immediately called his father.

"Anand, where are you? Why have you not resumed duty and why are you not answering the phone?" asked his anxious father.

Anand assumed that his parents had called the office as he had not answered their calls.

"Oh nothing, felt a little unwell. So, came back home. All is well."

"Shall I send your mother over to look after you?"

"No no, I am fine now. Don't worry," said Anand hurriedly, ending the conversation. *That was close,* he thought. But how long could he hide the facts from his parents?

Sitting in his drawing room, Anand felt strange. For the first time in his life he experienced a vacuum around himself. Suddenly he felt lost. It was as though he was placed in a balloon that floated in space, from where he could see people but could not communicate with them. A sense of panic, coupled with desperation, gripped him. He broke into a cold sweat and felt numb all over.

It was dark when Anand woke up to the sounds of children banging on the door of the adjacent flat. It took him a couple of minutes to come to his senses. He pulled himself up and staggered to the wash basin. Pouring cold water over his face, he tried to fight the sense of desperation. Just then, the ring on his mobile phone startled him. He walked back to the drawing room and with trembling hands lifted the phone from the table.

"Anand, are you alright?" enquired a familiar voice.

"Yes, yes. I am fine," replied Anand, trying to figure out who was on the line.

"Are you sure? You answered on the twelfth call," complained the caller.

"I am busy right now. Will call you later," said Anand.

"Busy? With what?" demanded the caller.

"Later, later," said Anand.

"Wait. Don't disconnect. I am Amit calling from office. Deepak Mishra informed me about your visit," said the person on the line. "Look, Anand all I can say is that this will pass. Please don't do anything that will shatter your parents. I know it's a very difficult time for you, but please be brave. Promise me that you will not harm yourself," pleaded Amit.

Anand now recognized the voice. As he struggled to reply, the doorbell rang. "Anand, please open the door," said Amit over the phone.

Anand's dazed mind wondered whether Amit was talking on the phone or was with him in the room. The person at the door took the liberty of ringing the bell continuously. Trying to steady himself, Anand walked towards the door and mechanically opened it. His heart almost stopped beating when he saw his mother standing before him.

7

The Investigation

Suresh Sharma was abroad when the investigation into the fraud was underway. It was handled by his deputy, Praful Desai. When Suresh returned to office, his secretary briefed him about the case.

That day, Praful was away attending a seminar in Mumbai. So, Suresh decided to get a review on the happenings from the investigating team. He wanted to ensure that the complete sequence of events was conveyed to him. After lunch, the investigating team, excluding Kannan who was on leave, gathered in his cabin. Atul started the briefing.

"Sir, on being asked to go to the Treasury office, we met Amit Tandon, the Treasury head, who informed us that:

a. Dealer Anand Patel has been quoting foreign currency rates to M/s Adorn Exports Ltd (AEL) in four decimal places as against the bank's practice of two decimal places. The bank quotes four decimal rates only to very valued clients after taking sanction from the Rates Sanction Committee comprising the top management.

b. The rate report generated by the software is designed to print the rate in two decimal places. Hence, the rate quoted to AEL in four decimal places was not detected. When Anand Patel was on leave, an employee of AEL asked another dealer for a four-decimal quote, which prompted that dealer to check the rate report. Amit Tandon did not disclose the name of the dealer who unearthed this.

On learning this, we asked the software vendor to help us investigate the matter. It transpires that AEL has been banking with us for many years. Prior to 2008, the automation was in bits and parts. We checked the records from the day the new software was introduced i.e. April 29, 2008. AEL has been enjoying the four-decimal rate since October 15, 2008. We visited the AEL office and confirmed the same from their records. No other firms other than those with sanctions were quoted four decimal rates. Further, we obtained a report from the software team, detailing all authorizations by Anand. Other than the four-decimal quote, nothing else appeared amiss.

c. However, it was observed that there were a few transactions that had 'GM' marked on the extreme right side of the report. The software team informed that those were authorizations of wired Interbank Global Messaging. We had almost wound up the investigation, when, out of curiosity, we enquired with Amit about the wired Interbank Global Messaging system. He explained that most of the global financial institutions use the Interbank Global Messaging system to send and receive money in various currencies. The system has a global network that facilitates financial institutions to send and receive coded messages about monetary transactions in a regularized and secure environment. Money worth billions of dollars in various currencies is transferred on any working day to and from all countries in the world. Amit then enquired as to how we stumbled upon the messaging system. When we informed him about the transactions having the 'GM' marking, he called for the report. Amit was stunned to learn that Anand Patel had been sending messages through the Interbank Global Messaging system. He had been transferring dollars to various banks in New York.

Only the designated foreign exchange centers of banks are authorized to carry out such transfers on behalf of their clients, after obtaining the necessary documents and debiting the rupee amount from the client's account. Each and every transfer in foreign currency is then matched by the Matching Department to the corresponding debit to ensure that the bank has received the equivalent rupee amount. However, it transpired that twenty messages for USD remittances had been sent to USA without a corresponding debit in rupees, during the period September 2008 to December 2009. At first, Amit refused to believe this. According to him, it was impossible for such messages to go undetected. The software team was asked to recheck the report for any bug. The report was generated and regenerated a number of times. The result remained unchanged."

As he narrated the sequence of events to Suresh, the scenes in Amit's cabin flashed back in Atul's mind.

Amit had called his deputy, Rahul Kulkarni, and said, "Tomorrow is a Sunday, but we are coming to office along with the investigating team and software expert Tanmay. No one else should know about this."

The next day, Amit and Rahul entered the record room and pulled out the hard copies of the Interbank Global Messaging system messages. To their shock, they realized that Anand Patel had indeed sent the messages. But how could such messages go unnoticed was the question on top of Amit's mind. Definitely the Nostro account had been debited. Nostro account is an account maintained by a bank in a foreign country in their currency. For example, an account maintained by an Indian bank in the US in dollars is a Nostro account. All banks have systems in place to reconcile their accounts. Ensuring that for every outflow or inflow of foreign currency equivalent rupee amount is received from or paid to the clients is the only job of the Matching Team. Then how did this happen? Obviously, someone from the Matching Team had been hand in glove with Anand.

"Still, this is not possible," said Amit.

"Tanmay, give me a report of all such messages sent by Anand," said Rahul.

"Some bug in the software perhaps," said someone from the investigation team.

"God help us in that case," said Amit.

"Rahul, we have to recall the scenario of 2008. When did we go live on this software? Was it directly from manual to mechanized? Or did

we have something in between? Such things are possible only during the transition period," said Amit.

"Sir, we will have to talk to someone who was here in 2008 and is well-versed with the manual as well as the computerized system," replied Rahul.

"Yes, but what if he had been a party to the fraud," remarked Amit.

"Maybe, but we have to find out the scenario that prevailed then," said Rahul.

"Rahul, let's try and talk to Anna D'Souza. She worked in this department for many years and as I know her personally, I can vouch for her."

"Where is she posted now?"

"She quit a couple of years back."

"How do we find her?"

"Ask Sudha Nair. Tell her a common friend wants her phone number. And don't worry, Sudha is too refined to enquire about the common friend."

Half an hour later, Amit was talking to Anna. "Anna, I know you stay close to Connaught Place. Do me a favor. Can you come over to the office? And keep this confidential. I shall answer all your questions once you come over here."

An hour later, Anna was in the office. Amit briefed her about the messages and asked her about the transition from the old software to the core computerized system. Anna reflected for some time. She then recalled, "This must have been around 2006 when the bank switched over to a new software. But even then, branches were not connected to a common server. The Matching Department worked on an independent *software. Later in 2008, there was a major problem before migrating to the core banking software. The old entry Matching Software failed to boot. The backup drives were also not readable. I vividly remember that day. Initially, we were all confident that the IT guys would find a way out. But after a week of trying they gave up. To make matters worse, we realized that no hard copies had been taken.*

Obviously, there was panic. Where does one start from? The blame games started. When there was no option left, the main office was informed. At the same time, it was ensured that the details were not leaked for fear of various repercussions. A select team was formed, which built a base and started the entry matching work. It took about two years to clear the mess. In the meantime, the entire bank was migrating to the latest software."

"Anna, can you tell me whether Anand Patel was here in 2008?" asked Amit.

"You mean that boy from Surat? He had just joined the bank then."

"Was he involved with the Matching Team?"

"No, I don't think so. Anyway, it was so messy then, with so many staff members around and the manual records strewn all over."

"Anna, thanks a lot. I am sure you will keep all this confidential."

"Don't worry. But do tell me the final outcome."

"After Anna left, Amit spoke to Praful from the audit department and they decided to report the matter to the CEO of the bank," said Atul and completed his narrative.

After Atul finished, Suresh closed his eyes and ruminated on the narrative. It intrigued him as to how the curiosity about the 'GM' marking on a few transactions had unfolded a financial fraud that implicated Anand Patel. The investigating team members were not aware of Anand's meeting with Deepak. Suresh did not think it was necessary to inform them. He also felt that the investigating team had completed their task. Whether or not Anand Patel was guilty was beyond their assignment.

"I suppose you can close this investigation. In case any clarification is required, I shall consult Atul," Suresh told the investigating team.

8

The Clarifications

After the investigation team left, Suresh ruminated over all that he had heard. He felt that he needed some clarifications on the working of forex transactions. He decided to meet his friend Arnav Ghosh, who worked in the forex department of another bank, for dinner, to understand how forex transactions worked.

"Arnav, give me an idea of how a bank sends money abroad and how one matches the entries," said Suresh.

"Suresh, you are supposed to be an authority on this. What's the matter?" asked Arnav.

"Something serious has happened. Just want to refresh myself on the topic."

"Alright, let's suppose you want to send some money, say 100 dollars, to a friend in the US. You approach your bank and tell them that you have to make an outward remittance of 100 dollars. If the purpose is permitted by FEMA/RBI, the bank will ask you to fill in a form, debit your account, convert the rupees to dollars by applying the TT selling rate prevailing at that time and then send an Interbank Global Messaging system message to its correspondent bank in the US where your bank is maintaining its Nostro account. On receipt of the Interbank Global Messaging system message, the correspondent bank will credit your friend's account by debiting your bank's account with them. Conversely, if your friend has to send you money from the US, his bank will debit his account in dollars and credit your bank's Nostro account and send an Interbank Global Messaging system message to your bank. On receiving the message, your bank will convert the dollars into rupees by applying the TT buying rate prevailing at that time and credit the rupees into your account."

"Is it possible to send an Interbank Global Messaging system message without an underlying debit transaction?" asked Suresh.

"It's possible. Sometimes the transaction fails due to technical problems but the message is sent. Banks have systems in place to check such things. At the end of the day, all correspondent banks send a statement of accounts to the bank, which then matches all the entries with their own books."

Arnav noticed that Suresh's attention was not on his food. He was tempted to ask Suresh the cause of his worry, but refrained from doing so.

9

The FIR

Amit Tandon, Suresh Sharma and L Kannan were seated across the CEO in the latter's office. They had come to seek his permission to delay filing an FIR of fraud. After briefing the CEO on the facts of the case, they put forth their arguments for not filing the FIR immediately.

Amit began, "As per the records, Anand Patel has sent messages over the Interbank Global Messaging system without any underlying debit transaction. No person with an intent to defraud would do so using his own ID. Anand apparently does not know the procedure of sending messages and the messaging software is not loaded in the dealing room. Had it been Anand who had sent the messages, the Matching Team would have detected it.

Such a fraud was possible only by someone from the Matching Section. If an FIR is filed, Anand cannot enter the office and he will not be able to help in the investigation and the real culprit would go scot-free. If Anand is indeed the culprit, he will definitely fumble during the investigation and get caught."

The CEO was not convinced of this, but the fact that the persons in front of him were seasoned bankers who were putting up a united front stopped him from refusing flatly.

"I will give you a week's time to find the culprit or we file the FIR," the CEO said.

The trio walked out of the CEO's cabin and headed to Suresh's cabin.

"Anand Patel denies sending those messages. In that case, we have to find the culprit. How do we go about it?" said Suresh.

"As of now it seems to be the handiwork of someone from the Matching Team. But the question is, who can we trust to dig old graves?" said Amit.

After much deliberation, they decided to call Narendra Kamath who was in charge of the migration to the new software and also a member of the Matching Team in 2008.

"What if Narendra is the culprit?" remarked Suresh.

"Yes maybe, but he is the only person who can solve the mystery. If he himself is involved, his behavior will give him away. We must watch him keenly," said Amit.

Narendra Kamath

Narendra, who was now heading the Greater Kailash branch, joined them in half an hour. He was tall, handsome, in his early thirties, highly qualified, knowledgeable, computer-savvy and ambitious. He could charm one and all. His wife was an investment banker at another bank. Together they made a nice couple. They had no children.

Everyone observed Narendra keenly as he was briefed about the matter. *The surprise on his face appears genuine, but he may have rehearsed this a number of times. After all, he must have weighed the possibility of getting caught, if he is indeed the culprit,* thought Suresh to himself. But the others seemed convinced that Narendra was innocent.

"Narendra, what do you suggest?" asked Amit.

"I will have to look at all the messages sent, track the entries and their matching. Give me a day to do that. I don't think Anand could have done this. I do not remember him interacting with any member of the team," said Narendra.

After deliberating over the fraud with Amit and Suresh for half an hour, Narendra informed them that he had an important appointment at 4 p.m. and thus had to leave. He promised to join them the next day for further discussions.

10

More Suspects

The next day, Narendra was in the Treasury audit room. He had to go through the records to catch the culprit. The details of the fraudulent entries were given to him. He had been asked to prepare a plan for the investigation and report to Suresh Sharma, the audit chief. To avoid speculations on his presence at the Treasury, it was conveyed to those concerned that he was preparing a report to be submitted to the board.

After scrutinizing the record, Narendra concluded thus:

1. It was the work of a very observant and intelligent person. One who knew the workings of the forex department very well. Anand could not have pulled off such a smart move sitting in the dealing room.

2. It was six months after the special Matching Team was formed that the first message of $2000 was sent.

3. Under what circumstances was an Interbank Global Messaging system ID created for Anand Patel and that too with full powers?

4. But for the investigation into the four-decimal rate quote, the message fraud would have gone unnoticed.

5. Someone from the Matching Team was definitely involved. The messages were sent during the period the special team worked.

6. Or was the culprit from the software team? After all, the software team was required to understand how the manual systems worked in order to write the software. Also, only someone from the software team can create a login ID. But the Matching Team was working on a different software then.

Narendra then proceeded to create a profile of each member of the Matching Team. This is what it looked like.

Chandrashekhar Rai

Chandrashekhar Rai: In his early forties, average looking, married, with two school-going children who were doing well in studies. Intelligent, hardworking and well-behaved, with no apparent vices. An asset to the organization. Appears too good to be true. Though capable, he had never opted for a promotion.

Siddharth Malhotra

Siddharth Malhotra: In his late thirties, handsome, livewire, full of energy, has a school-going daughter and lives with his parents in a posh locality. Dresses well, enjoys good food and travel. It is a known fact that his grandfather had sold his ancestral property in Gurgaon and divided the proceeds equally among his three children, each of whom got a handsome amount. Siddharth's father had invested his share in residential and commercial properties and is enjoying rental income. Siddharth, being the only child, is comfortably placed. Though intelligent, he was not much inclined towards academics in his school and college days. Was a cricket buff, followed the game with great interest and wanted to become a cricketer himself, but lacked the required talent.

Nitin Guha

Nitin Guha: A Bengali, around forty or so years. Loves fish; fish is the center of most of his discussions. Easygoing, came to office, did his work, discussed fish and went home. Not much known about his family.

Ganesh Thaly

Ganesh Thaly: Goan, in his mid-thirties, has a school-going daughter, good at work, interested in all that happens in office. The boss's pet, he reports everything to the boss. If you hate a colleague and wish to convey something nasty to him, just call Ganesh, discuss it with him and rest assured that by evening the entire conversation would reach the colleague in question and a few others too. Called the Official Reporter. Beyond this, he can harm no one as he lacks the guts. Has an undying love for fish curry rice and constantly grumbles about its non-availability in Delhi.

Sonam Shah

Sonam Shah: Tall, good-looking and a snob. In her late forties, with a son and a daughter, both studying in the UK where her husband works. She is well off; but why give up a comfortable, well-paid job is her reason for staying back in India. Maintains very good rapport with all the bosses. Takes leave at least once a year to visit the UK and also as and when a member of her NRI family chooses to visit India. Behaves as if she is doing the bank a favor by attending office. A capable worker, but does not do beyond the allotted target. Why work more than what you are paid for, she reasons. Not liked much by her colleagues. Has an opinion on anything and everything under the sun. Loves to gather news from Ganesh.

Aditi Manav

Aditi Manav: Thirty-eight years, unmarried, slim, good-looking, charming, amicable and sharp. Colleagues always wonder why she is still single. Lives in a joint family in a spacious bungalow in Noida. Gets to office on time, does her job well and wraps work as soon as possible, though never before closing time.

11

The Route

Narendra tried to remember the scenario in 2007–2008, when the bank was only partially computerized. The system worked thus. The forex branches loaded their daily transactions from the branch system onto a CD. Their system had a program that copied the data in the required format onto the CD. The branches then sent the CD to the Treasury, where the data from the CD was copied on to the Matching Software. The Nostro statements were also loaded on the Matching Software. The entries were then matched by the computer operators by clicking on the entries.

All had been well till February 27, 2008. On February 28, 2008, the Matching Software server did not boot. The hardware and software engineers spent the entire day trying to locate the fault. A week went by. But there was still no progress. It was then decided to reload the software and start work from the last backup. But where was the backup disk? After a lot of searching and questioning, it transpired that the practice of taking backup had been done away with. Questions flew fast and thick. *Why, when and at whose instance?* But the questions had no answers.

When was the last backup taken? No one knew this. After a couple of days, a few disks were found. But only one of them was readable; it carried the backup of July 26, 2007. There was no option but to go back and redo everything. Needless to say, there was panic, blaming, cursing, bickering and a lot of bad blood. Memos were issued, increments were stopped and some people were given the pink slips too. The biggest lesson learnt was this:

computerization is a boon as long as everything works well and backups are available.

Rebuilding the data from July 26, 2007 was a Herculean task. The only solution was to get people to focus solely on the job. So, a special Matching Team was formed.

It took Narendra an entire day to work out a plan. He had a nagging suspicion that he too was a suspect. Just before closing hours, Narendra emailed his entire investigative plan to Amit, Suresh and Kannan.

It read thus:

1. Find out the details of the account to which the money was sent.

2. Find the mode of matching the entries. This can give a clue about the mindset of the culprit.

3. As the culprit has made money, scrutinize the accounts of all the suspects.

It was decided that Narendra would work with Atul Prabhu and Tanmay Gupta. Atul was asked to observe Narendra keenly.

A total of twenty messages had been sent with amounts ranging from $2000 to $3000, between September 2008 and December 2009. The amounts had been sent to five accounts, in five banks in the US, and none of the account was in the correspondent bank. Obviously, this was done to make detection difficult. Getting the details such as address and phone number of the beneficiary was difficult. Thus, action one of the plan drew a blank.

Action two of the plan involved finding the mode of matching the entries. The culprit was indeed a genius. He had found twelve very old entries where dollars had been received by the bank but had not been credited to anybody's account for want of complete details. Due to the software failure and the resultant commotion, nobody's attention was drawn to these entries. The culprit had used the reference number of such entries and the exact amount while sending the message to the correspondent bank. The remaining eight entries were matched to an Earthquake Relief Fund account, maintained with one of the forex branches, which received huge donations from the US. The Earthquake Relief Fund officials were not very organized in maintaining their books. Also, it was rumored that these officials were not very honest.

Obviously, the culprit was aware of this account. He or she had matched every fraudulent entry on the very day it appeared in the matching system, thus avoiding any suspicion. The culprit had also taken advantage of the fact that, in all the mess, an accurate one-to-one matching of all parameters was not possible. One had to take a pragmatic approach to complete the Herculean task. This meant the culprit was from the Matching Team.

With the help of Suresh, the accounts of all the six members of the Matching Team were tracked. Nothing irregular was observed. Undoubtedly, the culprit would have used an account with another bank.

Meanwhile, Anand, who was on compulsory leave, was getting restless. Being accused of a fraud and not having anything to occupy himself with felt like a punishment without being proven guilty. Every day he called up Amit and Suresh. After a few days, he pleaded with them to let him help find the culprit.

"How can you help?" retorted Amit.

"Only when I am at the scene, my mind will work. At present, I can't say anything," replied Anand.

Amit called Suresh and discussed the possibility of letting Anand assist the investigating team on a holiday. Suresh agreed to this.

So, Anand joined Narendra, Atul and Tanmay on Sunday at the Treasury office. After a briefing from Narendra about the latest developments, Anand went through the list of the messages. A total of $50,000 had been sent to five accounts in New York. All the beneficiaries had foreign names.

1. Mark Smith
2. Tom Spark
3. Timothy Lopez
4. Jose Martin
5. Daniel Brown

Anand jotted down the dates of the messages. If he could show that he was on leave on even one of these dates, he could prove his innocence. But he could not log into the HR software. He would have to request Narendra to check it the next day. As he sat sulking about it, Atul came to his rescue. He had the authority to access the HR software as an auditor.

After Atul checked the data, it became clear that Anand had been present on all the twenty dates when the remittance messages were sent. This left Anand dejected, but he was determined to prove his innocence. The next question was under whose ID were these entries matched. The software used back then was old and the different logins were not shown.

"Oh! Another dead-end!" exclaimed Anand. He then rested his head on the table. His head was abuzz with thoughts that made him feel dizzy. "Let's have lunch," he said.

The four men sauntered to a restaurant nearby.

"What will you have?" asked Narendra.

"You order anything," said everyone.

Narendra was confused. "Okay! What will you not have?" he asked.

Each of them told Narendra what they did not like. Finally, they settled for some pasta and fried rice.

Anand liked the way Narendra decided the lunch menu, using the process of elimination. Suddenly he smiled.

"What's the joke?" asked Atul.

"No joke. Thank you, boss, for giving me an idea on how to proceed further," said Anand addressing Narendra. "The elimination process..."

After returning to the audit room, Anand requested Atul to find out who from the Matching Team had been on leave on the dates the messages had been sent. That would rule out the absentees from the list of suspects.

A couple of hours passed, but there was no progress. All the members of the Matching Team had been present on the dates the messages were sent. Anand felt dejected again, but he tried to overcome the feeling. Narendra got a call from home and had to leave immediately. Atul took the opportunity to check Narendra's leave record. He too was present on all the twenty days. *So, Narendra could be the culprit too,* thought Atul. After a couple of hours, Atul and Tanmay started winding up for the day. Anand felt disappointed. He would not be able to join the team the next day. But he now had a fair idea of things.

After reaching home, Anand went through the dates and names over and over again. He wrote down the dates in various formats: dd-mm-yy, dd-mm-yyyy, dd-month-yy and dd-month-yyyy. Nothing came out of it, none of the dates revealed anything. It was past 1 a.m. when Anand got up with a start. The dates kept appearing again and again in front of his eyes. He feared that he would go crazy at this rate. He tried to sleep but could not. Suddenly, he remembered that on August 6, 2009, he had left office at 11 a.m., as his friend had been hospitalized after an accident. As he had already done a few deals, he could not be marked absent. He had to check the time of the message dated 06/08/2009. He would have to ask Atul for the time of the message. Probably this would prove his innocence.

12

The Connection

The next morning, Narendra, Atul and Tanmay were back in the audit room. Anand called Atul and asked for the timing of the message dated 06/08/2009. When Atul asked for the reason, Anand obliged. Half an hour later, Anand received a call from Atul. The time was 3.30 p.m. Anand was ecstatic. Atul cautioned him against sharing the information with the other team members. Anand guessed that Narendra too was a suspect.

In the meantime, Atul decided to list the leave period enjoyed by the six members of the Matching Team as well as Narendra. He tried to bring some connection between the leave period and the twenty dates. After keying in the data on an Excel sheet, he observed that the messages had been sent mostly after a person on leave had resumed duty. Shockingly, Narendra had taken only one day leave in all of 2008, four days in 2009 and ten days in 2010. He decided to discuss this with Amit before leaving office.

"Well, the leave records and dates of entries don't reveal anything. The culprit ensured that the messages were sent only when the quorum was full," said Atul.

"We will also have to find out who created Anand's ID or got it created in the Interbank Global Messaging system. Tanmay, can you find out please?" said Narendra.

Tanmay punched some commands on the computer and located the date. It was August 29, 2008. Atul immediately checked the HR software. He was shocked to see that all six members had been on leave that particular day. Narendra too had been on leave.

"That was the day road and rail traffic had come to a halt as it had rained continuously the previous night. Anand's ID in the Interbank Global Messaging system may have been created to send some interbank messages," said Narendra.

"Please elaborate, Narendra, as I don't understand," said Atul.

"Other than client transactions, there are transactions between banks. They are called interbank transactions. Banks trade in foreign currency, i.e. they buy and sell dollars to book a profit from exchange rate differences or fluctuations during the day. The date of settlement of such deals is different. On any particular day, the netting of such sales and purchases is done and the balance is required to be paid or received from the counter party bank with whom these deals have been done. There is a clearing house that handles this settlement for its member banks. But banks are required to pay dollars and receive rupees or vice versa, to the clearing house, for which an Interbank Global Messaging system message has to be sent to the correspondent bank. As most of the staff was on leave, Anand's ID was perhaps created as he was present on that day. As he stays nearby, he had attended office on that day," explained Narendra.

"Oh! Oh!" said Atul.

"Narendra, why would Anand share his password with anyone?" asked Atul.

Narendra reflected for some time and said, "Anand may not have shared his password. Generally, when an ID is created, the software team gives the password as ABCD or 12345, which should ideally be changed immediately on login. Anand may not have changed it."

"But why did Anand not get the ID deleted? How did the culprit learn about this?" asked Atul.

"Days such as 29/08/2008 are very rare and are discussed very much. During the next three to four days, the only topic of discussion was probably how the messages were sent, who sent them, how so and so gave instructions over the phone to log in and how they blundered and so on," replied Narendra.

The next couple of hours were spent scanning the record for some more clues.

"Narendra, let's check the dates of matching the entries with the leave record. Perhaps we can eliminate someone," said Atul.

Again, the culprit proved to be very clever. He had ensured that everyone had been present on those days.

Atul wanted to discuss a few things with Anand. He called up Anand and asked him to join them for lunch at 2 p.m. at a restaurant that was far away from the office, to ensure that Anand was not seen by his colleagues

At 2 p.m., Narendra, Atul and Tanmay met Anand for lunch.

"Anand, do you remember when your ID for messaging was created?" asked Atul.

Anand looked surprised. "Oh god! Why did this question not strike me?"

He reflected for about fifteen minutes and then said, "Yes, it had rained very heavily one day in 2008 and only a few of us had reached office. There were a few interbank messages to be sent for which my ID was created. I remember the interbank guy giving instructions over phone."

"Did you disclose your password to anyone?" asked Atul.

"To tell you the truth, I did not change the password. It was 12345 or something like that," said Anand.

"How did the culprit know that your ID was created?" asked Atul.

Anand tried to recall the events of those days. "I suppose the next day everyone knew. Everybody was discussing how the office managed to function. After all, we are in the Treasury of the bank," said Anand.

Narendra and Atul exchanged glances. This was exactly what Narendra had said. "My biggest mistake was I did not realize the importance of the ID. Now I am paying the price," said Anand.

"How come the message of 29/08/2008 did not appear in your report, Tanmay?" asked Atul.

"I was told to give the start date as September 1, 2008 as the data was running into many pages," said Tanmay.

The trio returned to the office after lunch. There was nothing much that could be done. Atul once again started tracking the accounts of all the six members. Nothing amiss was found. Amit dropped by to check on the progress. The trio informed him about the dead-end they had reached. Amit left without any comment. Atul followed him to his cabin.

"Sir, just have to inform you that Narendra has not availed himself of much leave during 2008, 2009 and 2010," said Atul.

"Nothing unusual, Atul. With all the mess around, nobody would have sanctioned him leave," said Amit.

"But everyone else in the Matching Team has taken leave," argued Atul.

"They were handpicked, Atul. They came from the other branches. They were the chosen ones. Nobody would have refused them leave. Call the others over. Let's see what else can be done," said Amit.

When Narendra and Tanmay joined them, Amit asked them, "Any suggestions?"

"Let's call for the telephone call data of all the six people," said Tanmay.

"Who will oblige? No FIR has been filed as yet," said Atul.

"Let's call for the phone data of our office. We may be able to trace something," suggested Tanmay.

"Even if you trace something, how will you know who made or received those calls?" said Amit.

"Narendra, as you have worked with these six people, can you shortlist a few suspects?" asked Atul.

"It won't be fair on my part to do that without any clues," argued Narendra.

"I suggest we call each of them separately and directly accuse him or her. Tell each one of them that we have proof against him/ her. The culprit will have to come forward and confess," suggested Atul.

"Atul, don't forget that the culprit is very clever. He or she will ask for proof. The only option now is tracing the five foreign accounts.

I don't want to use my contacts for such a thing, but I guess there is no choice. We shall meet after a couple of days. In the meantime, try something else to solve the mystery," concluded Amit.

As the trio walked out of Amit's office, Narendra saw Ganesh talking to someone. Hoping that Ganesh had not seen him, Narendra started walking in the opposite direction.

"Hello Narendra," shouted Ganesh.

"Hello Ganesh," replied Narendra.

"Narendra, so good to see you. Have you been transferred back to this office?" asked Ganesh excitedly.

"No, just preparing a report for the board. How are you Ganesh?" asked Narendra.

"Good, good. Had come to Connaught Place to meet a client, so thought might as well catch up with some colleagues here," replied Ganesh.

Now the whole world will know that I am preparing a report, thought Narendra. *God knows what else Ganesh will spread around. He knows almost all the people in and around the building, from the security guards and liftmen to drivers and tea vendors.*

The same night, as Anna was walking home, she received a call from Ganesh.

"Hi Anna, how are you?"

"Ganesh, what a surprise! How are you?"

"Today I had been to the Treasury department. The security guard told me you were there one Sunday. What's up?"

Anna's heart skipped a beat. *Of all the people, the security guard tells Ganesh about my visit. Well, who else but Ganesh would go around talking to anyone and everyone,* thought Anna.

"Well, I was passing by when I saw Amit parking his car. Just went up to say hello," said Anna.

"I also met Narendra today in Treasury. He is preparing some report for the board," said Ganesh.

"What else?" asked Anna.

Ganesh shared all the latest gossip with Anna. Then, promising to keep in touch, he hung up the phone.

Anna immediately called Amit to tell him about Ganesh's phone call.

"Amit, this is an emergency. By morning, the entire Matching Team will know about my visit to your office on Sunday and Narendra's report for the board. The culprit may put two and two together and be forewarned."

"Is there a remote possibility of Ganesh being the culprit?" Amit was quick to react.

"No. According to me, he lacks the guts required to defraud a bank," observed Anna.

"In that case Anna, call him up and ask him to keep his mouth shut. Also, tell me if he can be of any help to us. People who gossip are a storehouse of information."

"Yes, he can provide us a lot of information and can be helpful in getting the latest updates."

"Okay, call him over to your house tomorrow evening. I too shall come over if it's okay with your family."

"No problem Amit, my husband would be glad to meet you after so long. So tomorrow at 7 p.m. I shall message you my address."

After his conversation with Anna, Amit called his contacts in various banks to try and gather as much information as possible about the five beneficiary accounts to which the money had been transferred. The general response was that such a job would take time. Amit wondered how many of them were sincere and how many were just buying time.

The next evening, Amit got information about three beneficiary accounts of which two were closed. Neither the address nor the contact number of these accounts could be found. The account of Daniel Brown was still running. One of Amit's contacts had been sincere enough to trace the five credits to the account. The money credited to the account had been immediately transferred to an eWallet. Before Amit could ask him anything more, the contact told him that no further information could be gathered. The name of the eWallet was not mentioned in the statement. Amit sincerely thanked his contact. At last, he had managed to get some clue.

Amit reached Anna's place at 7.15 p.m. After meeting Anna's husband and the other family members, Amit was taken to the study room where Ganesh was browsing through a magazine. As soon as he saw Amit, he rushed to shake hands with him. Ganesh seemed thrilled like a small boy who had been promised an adventure.

"Anna, have you told him anything?" enquired Amit.

"No, we were waiting for you," said Anna.

"Ganesh, can I trust you to keep this meeting confidential?" asked Amit.

"Oh yes, my lips are sealed," said Ganesh.

"Do you know the penalty for opening your mouth? I will ensure that you are posted as far away as possible and for the longest period possible," threatened Amit.

Amit hated himself for threatening Ganesh, but he had no other option. He then proceeded to tell Ganesh about the fraud, revealing as little information as possible. Ganesh's expressions changed from excitement to that of shock. After asking some questions, he became a bit contemplative.

"Ganesh, give us any information that you think will be of help to us in solving the case," said Amit.

"Positively sir, I shall do all that I can," assured Ganesh.

The meeting was over by 8.30 p.m. Amit dropped Ganesh at the nearest metro station and proceeded home. He had to do his homework on eWallet.

Ganesh was on top of the world. At last, his inquisitive nature had brought some excitement to his life. The Treasury head of the bank had asked him to participate in the nabbing of a culprit! He could not help feeling good about himself. After all those years of receiving barbs for being such a nosy parker, he had finally got an opportunity to be a hero.

13

The eWallet

Amit searched the internet for 'eWallet'. He gathered the following information.

An eWallet works much like an individual's cash kept in a purse online. It is an online prepaid account where one deposits money in advance, to be used when required. It can be funded through a debit/credit card or a transfer from a bank account. Users can then shop online for a variety of products or pay their utility bills using this eWallet. They can also send money to anyone with a valid cell number.

Various websites detailed the actual working of the eWallet and the benefits and risks associated with it. The only thing that Amit gathered was that, by using an eWallet, the culprit had tried to complicate the tracking of the money that had been fraudulently sent out. Online shopping had just picked up in India. So, way back in 2008, very few people were familiar with the concept of the eWallet. Obviously, someone having connections overseas could have found ways to use it. Amit had to look for such an employee the next day. Somehow, he could not digest the concept of someone defrauding the bank for shopping. *There must be some other use of the eWallet,* thought Amit.

Siddharth Malhotra and Sonam Shah went overseas at least once a year. *One of these two could have definitely been involved,* thought Amit. *And what about Narendra? His wife was an investment banker and she too went abroad often.*

The next day, Amit called Atul to his cabin. Together they went through all the personal accounts of Siddharth and Sonam, but they had no luck. Then they scanned Narendra's account, again with no success. Amit then decided to scan the accounts of the remaining members.

As they went through Aditi's account, Amit noticed that many cheques had been issued to various electronic stores. This definitely attracted his attention. From what he had heard about Aditi, he imagined her to be a mundane person. *What electronic purchases had she been making,* he wondered. *Had she been gifting electronic items to members of her family?* He decided to check with Anna. However, Anna could not help him on this. "Can you check with Ganesh if he can throw some light on this?" enquired Amit, with a reminder to keep everything confidential.

Amit was getting restless. Many days had passed with no clue in sight. He wondered what to do next. According to him, the possible suspects were Sonam, Siddharth and possibly Narendra too. What about Aditi? He had never suspected Anand of sending the messages. Later at night, he called Anand and told him about Daniel Brown and the transfer to an eWallet account.

"Anand, way back in 2008–09, not many were familiar with the eWallet expect for some academic knowledge. Can you try and make some sense of it?" said Amit.

"Sure sir, after all, I am saving my own skin in the process," replied Anand.

Anand immediately started browsing the internet. He sat up the whole night reading whatever was available on eWallet. He also made some notes to send to Amit.

An eWallet can make online shopping easier and faster. eWallets are also used by artists, writers, programmers, freelancers and others to accept payments from their clients across the globe. Expats use them to transfer money between their accounts in different countries.

Many eWallet companies are regulated by the UK's statutory authority FSA and they have millions of customers around the globe. Most Indians use them for transactions not related to gambling, thus making it convenient for banks in India to deal with eWallet companies. In the US, an eWallet is used primarily for online gambling.

Gambling is defined as an activity that involves playing a game for stakes or betting on an uncertain result. Lotteries, casino games, poker and sports betting are various forms of gambling.

Sports betting is the activity of predicting sports results and placing a bet on the outcome.

Many European gambling sites allow Indians to bet online. An eWallet can be used to deposit money in an online gambling site. Gamblers also find it easy to transfer funds from one betting site to another by getting their winnings credited to their eWallet as their bank account statement shows only the name of the eWallet and not the gambling site.

14

The Probable Suspects

The trio Narendra, Atul and Tanmay gathered every day in the audit room at the Treasury looking for leads to nail the culprit.

"There is nothing more we can do. Atul and Tanmay, any suggestions?" asked Narendra.

"No, nothing," said Atul.

Atul wondered whether Narendra knew that Amit had been looking into everyone's account. After an hour, the three of them went to meet Amit, but he was busy. Later in the day, Amit walked into the audit room.

"Any developments?" he enquired.

The three men shook their heads in the negative.

"Well then Narendra, tell me who you suspect the most and why?" asked Amit.

Narendra hesitated as he was not sure whether he should open up in front of Atul and Tanmay. He tried to buy time by saying he would prepare a report and then discuss the matter.

Amit returned to his cabin. His mind kept going back to Aditi's account. He called Anna and asked her to tell him all that she knew about Aditi. Anna did not have much to share about Aditi. "Then who can help regarding this?" enquired Amit. Anna promised to find out more and get back to him. Amit also requested Anna to list out the members of the Matching Team on the basis of susceptibility—from the 'most likely' to the 'least likely'. He asked her to request the same from Ganesh. As Amit kept down the phone, Narendra entered his cabin. Amit motioned him to take a seat.

"I did not want to discuss this in front of Atul and Tanmay. But I cannot bring myself to suspect anyone without any proof or for that matter even a clue," said Narendra.

"But someone has actually defrauded the bank," remarked Amit.

"Yes, but we have not found anything. Probably you are suspecting me too. But I know I am innocent. Thus, without proof I cannot name anyone," said Narendra, emphatically.

Amit was stunned for a minute. Was his suspicion showing or was Narendra just making a general remark, he wondered.

"Okay, we shall carry on the investigation and see what happens," concluded Amit.

After Narendra left the cabin, Amit called Suresh and requested him to scrutinize the Assets and Liabilities statements submitted by the six members of the Matching Team and that of Narendra too, from 2008 to 2010 (all bank officers are required to submit their Assets and Liabilities statement every year to their employer).

Meanwhile, Anna contacted her friend Poonam Joshi, who stayed in Aditi's locality. Poonam's sister was Aditi's classmate. According to Poonam, Aditi had been a normal girl in school, never in the limelight for either good or bad reasons. She appeared to be contented with herself. Nothing much was known about her likes and dislikes. She lived in a joint family. The older generation ran a family business manufacturing sports goods. The younger generation was mostly into jobs.

As requested by Amit, Anna prepared a chart of the most probable suspects.

MEMBER	ANNA'S OPINION	GANESH'S OPINION
Chandrashekhar Rai	Could be a suspect. Has the required intelligence. Never gets into anyone's bad books.	Chandrashekhar can never do such a thing. Basically, a simpleton at heart.
Siddharth Malhotra	Very much a suspect. His lifestyle can always do with some extra money. Probably purchasing some property abroad.	Siddharth need not do such a thing. Has plenty of money to throw around.
Nitin Guha	No way a suspect. Nitin is too laidback to undertake such a risk. One of those people who wants a life without hassles.	Cannot commit such a crime. Though intelligent, is not the type to take pains.
Sonam Shah	Ruled out. Apparently, everything falls in place. Family is overseas whom she visits often. Snobbish, arrogant and has the brains and capability to execute a fraud, yet her integrity is beyond doubt.	Yes, she could be the culprit. Even after leaving Treasury, she keeps enquiring with me about what's going on there.
Aditi Manav	Impossible. Is fairly well off, not many wants and desires. A contented soul.	Maybe. After all, still waters run deep.

As requested by Amit, Suresh went through the Asset and Liability statement of all the members of the Matching Team. He found nothing unusual. Everyone had reported their assets as house, car, investments in various financial instruments, and furniture and fixtures. All six of them had reported housing and vehicle loans. Only Aditi had shown sizable investments in electronic items. *She is probably very meticulous in classifying items under proper heads,* thought Suresh. People generally clubbed such items under 'furniture and fixtures'.

Amit was excited on hearing that Aditi had reported substantial investments in electronic items. On enquiring with Suresh whether she had reported any property, he learnt that Aditi owned a flat in the same society where she stayed. Amit shared the information with Anna and asked her to gather some more information. "Not a problem," said Anna. She could depend on her friend Poonam for more information on Aditi.

After gathering the requisite information, Anna called Amit to inform him that Aditi's flat was very close to the bungalow she lived in. The children of the joint family frequented the flat with Aditi. One of them had very excitedly described in detail the various electronic toys and games that their aunt's flat had and how their aunt was an expert in most of the games. The children had fondly named the flat 'the den.' On hearing this, Amit wondered whether Aditi had a split personality. Her colleagues had described her to be a very sedate person. He thought he was probably right in suspecting her.

In the meantime, pressure was mounting on Suresh and Amit from their higher officials. Report the fraud to the police, they advised. But Amit once again succeeded in buying some more time for the investigation.

15

The Beneficiaries

There were five beneficiaries of the remittances totaling $50,000. Amit asked Atul and Tanmay to surf the internet for information on these beneficiaries. Mark Smith, Tom Spark, Timothy Lopez, Jose Martin and Daniel Brown.

The five names were so common that it wasn't easy to dig up information on them. Atul and Tanmay made brief notes. There were lawyers, doctors, engineers, scientists, writers, teachers and musicians under those names. One Jose Martin had got into a brawl in London in 2008. Timothy Lopez from San Francisco had applied for a patent for an instrument designed by him. A Mark Smith from New York had traveled on his bike for more than six months, touring the whole of the US. Another Mark Smith from Argentina spoke of his earlier birth in Brazil. Tom Spark of Columbia was caught collecting donations for a fake organization in March 2009. The notes ran into ten pages. Amit patiently went through the notes. Only one detail caught his fancy. Timothy Lopez of New York was arrested in November 2011 for using his bank account to receive money from punters.

"Get me a news report on this," Amit told Atul.

Atul dutifully printed out the report.

Timothy Lopez used his bank account to receive money from people overseas interested in sports betting. He also managed to convince many friends and acquaintances to receive such monies in their accounts. He ensured that the amount per transaction was small so as not to attract attention. He paid them a commission and promised to enrich them further.

The money thus received was sometimes withdrawn and sometimes transferred to eWallets. The police are investigating further.

Amit was excited but tried to appear businesslike. As Atul and Tanmay were unaware of the transfer of money from Daniel Brown's account to the eWallet, they could not make the connection. *Who was the punter among the six?* thought Amit. On his way back home, Amit called Anna.

"Anna, is there a sportsperson in Aditi's family?"

"Don't know, will have to find out. A huge joint family with so many youngsters will probably have a sportsperson. But tell me what exactly do you mean by a sportsperson?"

"A player or a sports lover..."

"Amit, why so much interest in Aditi's family?"

"Just a hunch. Could be a false lead. But do check and tell me."

Now that's difficult, thought Anna. She had lied to Poonam that there was a matrimonial alliance for Aditi and that was the reason for all the questions about Aditi and her family. Then suddenly Anna remembered that the Manav family sent all their children to the CAGS High School. It was like their family school; three generations of the family had passed out from it. It was a known fact that CAGS school gave a lot of emphasis to sports. Surprisingly, football, and not cricket, was the school's most favored sport. Anna surfed the internet on the CAGS football team and found two Manav boys in it. She promptly informed Amit about this.

16

Sports Betting

Amit wondered how to proceed with all the information he had gathered. Was there any connection or was he simply making absurd assumptions, he pondered. He then decided to do some research on sports betting. He found the revelations very interesting.

One who places a bet is called a **punter**. One who takes bets on sporting events or other events is called a **bookie or bookmaker**. Betting is illegal in many countries. Even in countries where betting is legal, some illegal betting syndicates offer better odds, thus tempting the punters.

Anything and everything can be betted upon.

Who will score first?

Who will win?

What will be the final score?

What will be the number of goals?

How many yellow cards will be issued?

How many red cards will be given?

Betting odds: Odds are the probability or the chance of a certain outcome in an event expressed numerically. Betting odds tell you the likelihood of a certain outcome in an event and consequently the amount of money that can be won on placing the bet.

Decimal odds: These are mostly used in Europe and are also called European odds. Hundred divided by the chance of happening as a % gives the decimal odds. For example, in a match between teams Y and Z, if the chance of team Y winning is 80%, then the decimal odd is 100/80 =1.25. In a decimal odd of 1.25, if one places a bet of €100 and wins, he or she will get back €100 x 1.25 = €125, thus making a profit of €25. Decimal odds always include the unit stake. The bigger the number in decimal odds, the higher is the return.

Fractional odds: These are used mostly by UK bookmakers. These are expressed by two numbers separated by a slash. X/Y. Two numbers separated by a slash is a fractional betting odd. Probability % = $Y/(X+Y)$. Thus, 9/1 is calculated as $1/(9+1)$ = 0.10, which means that the chance of the event happening is 10%. 4/1 is calculated as $1/(4+1)$ = 0.20 which means the chance of the event happening is 20%. Fractional odds represent profit. 4/1 means £4 for every £1 staked. Thus, X/Y means for every value of Y that you bet, you will win X+ return of your stake.

Why do people bet/gamble? Taking risk excites many people. It gives them an adrenaline rush. Gambling takes them away from their mundane, unexciting life. Some think it's fashionable to gamble. Many think it's an easy way to make money, not realizing it's a fast track to disaster. For many, it's an addiction.

How illegal betting works: The illegal betting industry must operate in such a manner that it does not get caught. Hence, all transactions must necessarily be in cash. There is a hierarchy in the setup. Only the lowest rung of the ladder is visible. They are the bookies who take bets from the punters. They get the odds from the next rung, who in turn get in touch with the higher level in the chain. Every level knows only the immediate next rung on the ladder. The people at the highest level are the ones with power and clout. The biggest fallout of betting is match fixing. Bribes and threats are the tools of match fixing. While money can tempt the corrupt players and managers, the team owners can easily threaten players to lose a match for betting gains.

Amit found the topic of betting very fascinating. He was reminded of his earlier driver Madhav, who had once narrated the wrestling scenario in his village. Madhav was a fatherly figure to one and all. Though he was only in his forties, he treated everyone like his younger brother or sister. He often spoke about his village. Wrestling was a sport widely played in and around his village. Inter-village competitions were known to be held since many decades. Such competitions were held during winter and were celebrated as festivals. Everyone loved to bet on the outcome of these competitions. The bets were harmless and never involved money.

The winners of the bets were treated to lavish meals. All this changed when a few villagers had guests from overseas, who introduced the concept of betting with money. Slowly, more and more villagers were tempted to get into betting. As the stakes grew, so did the involvement of the local goons who started threatening some of the wrestlers to lose matches. Thus, match fixing came into being. Initially, the villagers were shocked when the better players lost. Later, when the truth came out, there were clashes and bitterness among the villagers. This soon sounded the death-knell on the sport itself.

For the next couple of days, Amit continued surfing the net after office hours. He still could not connect the dots. He read the notes sent by Anand on eWallets again. He concluded that the culprit had used the eWallet for sports betting.

17

Face to Face

Suresh telephoned Amit enquiring about the progress in the investigation.

"I shall zero in on the suspects in a day or so," said Amit.

After Suresh hung up, Amit became pensive. *I can't go on researching forever,* he thought. He decided to wind up the day by 5 p.m. and then work on the suspects based on all the information he had gathered.

After dinner that night, he pulled out the chart wherein Anna and Ganesh had listed their observations of the Matching Team members.

MEMBER	ANNA'S OPINION	GANESH'S OPINION
Chandrashekhar Rai	Could be a suspect. Has the required intelligence. Never gets into anyone's bad books.	Chandrashekhar can never do such a thing. Basically, a simpleton at heart.
Siddharth Malhotra	Very much a suspect. His lifestyle can always do with some extra money. Probably purchasing some property abroad.	Siddharth need not do such a thing. Has plenty of money to throw around.
Nitin Guha	No way a suspect. Nitin is too laidback to undertake such a risk. One of those people who wants a life without hassles.	Cannot commit such a crime. Though intelligent, is not the type to take pains.
Sonam Shah	Ruled out. Apparently, everything falls in place. Family is overseas whom she visits often. Snobbish, arrogant and has the brains and capability to execute a fraud, yet her integrity is beyond doubt.	Yes, she could be the culprit. Even after leaving Treasury, she keeps enquiring with me about what's going on there.
Aditi Manav	Impossible. Is fairly well off, not much wants and desires. A contented soul.	Maybe. After all, still waters run deep.

Amit then compared this with Narendra Kamath's chart, which carried the characteristics of the erstwhile team members. He decided to use his logic and gut instinct to prepare the final list of suspects.

To him, Chandrashekhar and Nitin did not appear as fraudsters. Siddharth and Sonam went abroad regularly; so, they could qualify as suspects. Aditi's interest in electronic items and video games, coupled with the fact that her family was interested in sports, put her in the list of suspects.

Finally, Amit Tandon zeroed in on Sonam Shah, Siddharth Malhotra and Aditi Manav as the suspects. The culprit had to be one of them, he felt. He discussed this with Suresh.

"But how do we go about nailing the culprit?" asked Suresh.

"We have no option but to confront them," said Amit.

"Confront them?" exclaimed Suresh.

"Yes. We will call them over to the main office and confront them separately. We then directly accuse them of the fraud," said Amit.

"But that's cruel and unfair to the innocent," remarked Suresh.

"I agree. But there's no other way. The bosses are pressurizing me for an outcome," said Amit.

"What happens if all of them deny any involvement?" asked Suresh.

"We will then tell them that we are handing over the case to the police," countered Amit.

Suresh reflected over their conversation.

"Amit, we have two women among the suspects. I am not comfortable with the confrontation suggestion," said Suresh.

"Better we confront them than the police," said Amit.

Suresh reluctantly agreed to the confrontation.

"Amit, we better have a lady officer in the room while confronting. Also, let's record the whole thing. Don't want this to backfire with allegations of sexual harassment."

"Yes, that's a very valid point. Also, we must keep the higher-ups informed about this," said Amit.

Amit and Suresh decided to do the confrontation the following Saturday morning. After confirming that all the three suspects were present in their respective branches, confidential sealed envelopes were sent to them with a copy to the branch heads. The three of them were asked to report to the main office. It was ensured that the envelopes carrying the instructions were received by them in a staggered manner and not at the same time.

Aditi received it at 10 a.m., Sonam at 11 a.m. and Siddharth at noon. They were instructed to report to the Customer Service department so that they would not be alarmed immediately.

Aditi reported at the Customer Service department at 10.45 a.m. Usha Atre, a senior lady executive at the department, casually asked her a few questions on the quality of customer service in her branch. She then asked Aditi to accompany her to the mini conference room.

Sonam reached the main office at noon. She was asked to fill in a questionnaire on the customer service initiatives taken at her branch. She was then asked to write a note on how customer service could be improved. Unsuspectingly and enthusiastically, Sonam started writing.

After Siddharth reached the department, he was taken to the recreation room on the sixth floor and asked to fill the questionnaire on customer service. He was taken aback.

"You called me to fill up this?" he asked the person accompanying him.

"I have not called you. I am only following instructions," was the reply that Siddharth received.

"Who gave you these instructions?" enquired Siddharth.

"The Customer Service department officials."

"Why only me?"

"No. A number of others have also been called."

"And where are these others?"

"Many have completed it and gone. The others are on their way."

Siddharth could not concentrate on the questions. Was the bank reducing staff, he wondered. *This is how organizations go about giving the pink slip,* he thought. Just a couple of weeks ago, he had heard about a few banks laying off employees. This was how the so-called downsizing was done. He kept asking the official who was with him what was going on, but the official pleaded ignorance.

"Please fill up the questionnaire" was all Siddharth got from him.

To buy some time, Siddharth asked for water. He then feigned dizziness. The official accompanying him called someone over phone. Immediately, a doctor walked in. Seeing the doctor, Siddharth was sure that the bank was downsizing. Organizations took ample precaution while giving the pink slip. They always had doctors, counselors and the police around. The doctor found nothing wrong with Siddharth. He called for some orange juice and asked Siddharth to have some.

The persons accompanying Sonam and Siddharth had been asked to keenly observe them and report their observations. Sonam was unaware of the fact that she was being observed. But Siddharth sensed something amiss. He kept looking around, trying to get a clue as to what was going on.

Aditi's confrontation began. She was taken to a cabin called the M cubicle on the top floor. It was big enough to seat eight to ten people. There was an oval table at the center with chairs around it. Amit was sitting at one end, facing the door. Aditi was asked to sit at the other end. Suresh sat on Amit's right and Usha, the lady who had accompanied Aditi, occupied the chair on Amit's left. Aditi noted an elderly man next to Suresh. She was not aware that he was Dr Trehan, a psychologist. Aditi wished everyone and sat down in anticipation.

"Well Aditi, we are planning to send a few employees from the bank abroad for a ten-day workshop on interbank messaging. This interview is a part of the selection process. Just relax and answer our questions," said Amit.

Aditi's face was expressionless. She just nodded her head.

"What is your favorite video game?" asked Amit.

"I don't play video games," answered Aditi.

"Your favorite sport?"

"None."

"Your hobbies?"

"None."

"Aditi, don't hesitate. You must be having some hobby," prodded Amit.

"No, and I am not interested in going for any workshop."

"What are the odds in the Chelsea versus Tottenham game to be played tomorrow?"

Aditi looked astonished for a second before she answered, "I don't know what you are talking about."

"Whom should I wager on—Chelsea or Tottenham?"

Aditi's face was blank.

"Aditi, you are familiar with all this. Who are Daniel Brown, Mark Smith and Tom Spark?"

Aditi did not utter a word.

"Aditi, you have been sending Interbank Global Messaging system messages without any underlying transaction. You have defrauded the bank to the tune of Rs 25 lacs. Admit it."

"I don't know what you are talking about."

Suresh too tried to convince Aditi to admit her transgression. But she remained adamant. Half an hour later, Usha accompanied Aditi to the adjoining room.

Next, Sonam was brought to the M cubicle and was asked to sit on the same chair that Aditi had occupied. Amit started with the same introduction.

"We are planning to send a few employees from the bank abroad for a ten-day workshop on interbank messaging. This interview is a part of the selection process. Just relax and answer the questions."

"Which country is it? The UK?" was Sonam's immediate response. As she had worked with Amit when he was at a junior level, she looked at him as a friend.

"Yes, in fact it is UK. How did you know?" asked Amit.

"I was just guessing. In fact, I am glad it is UK. My family lives there."

"What is your family doing in the UK?"

"My children are studying there and my husband runs a business there."

"What business?"

"He is into textiles. He and his partners import textiles from India."

"What's the annual turnover like?"

"No idea, but the profits are decent enough to live an adequate life in the UK."

"What do you mean by adequate life?" probed Amit.

"We have enough money for necessities and a few luxuries like going on a holiday every year, eating out, shopping and all that."

"In that case, why have you chosen to stay back and work in India?" enquired Amit.

"Well, I am planning to shift there. The children went there a couple of years back. We were not sure if they would like the place. But they have settled down comfortably. So, I may move there soon."

"Is education very expensive in the UK?"

"Oh yes, it costs a bomb, especially if you convert the pounds to rupees."

"Sonam, have you heard about sports betting?"

"Yes, I have heard about that from my husband. He and his friends keep discussing it. It's very popular in the UK."

"Is that the reason why you sent Interbank Global Messaging system messages to the US without any transactions backing the messages?" enquired Amit.

"Interbank Global Messaging system messages? Yes, I do know how to send those messages."

"So, you sent Interbank Global Messaging system messages amounting to Rs 25 lakhs when you were at the Treasury office in the Matching Team?" questioned Amit.

"No, no. These messages are sent by the branches."

"Sonam, you have defrauded the bank by sending messages from the Treasury without debiting any account," accused Amit.

"Defrauded. Who? Me? I don't understand what you are saying."

"Don't you know Daniel Brown and Mark Smith?" Amit questioned.

"No, I don't know anyone by those names."

"What about Tom Spark?" probed Amit.

"No, I don't know who Tom Spark is. In fact, I don't understand what's going on. First you ask about my family and then say I have defrauded the bank. Is this some psychological test? Are you trying to test my reaction under stress?"

Amit and Suresh noticed that Sonam was absolutely calm. There was no sign of disbelief, stress or anger. They were confused. Was Sonam acting calm and innocent or was she actually unaware of the fraud? They looked at each other and nodded as if they were in agreement to confront her further.

"Sonam, we are handing you over to the police," said Suresh.

"Police? For what? Can you please tell me what's going on? Is this an interview or some kind of drama? And don't threaten me. I am not scared."

"Sonam, the fact is that someone has been sending Interbank Global Messaging system messages from the Treasury without any underlying transaction. That someone has also matched the entries very cleverly. We are searching for that culprit," elaborated Amit.

"Oh! And just because my family is in the UK, you think it is me. Go ahead and hand me over to the police. I am totally innocent. So, I am not scared."

Amit and Suresh were taken aback. They had heard that Sonam was a very confident person, but they had not expected such a reaction.

"Okay. Can you think over it and tell us who could be the culprit?" asked Suresh.

"No! But even if I have to make a wild guess, I would need some more details of this pot boiler."

After being briefed about the fraud, Sonam was accompanied by a lady officer to the library.

Next, Siddharth was brought to the interrogation room. The minute he entered the room, he was sure that this was the final lap of the pink slip process.

Before anyone else could speak, he said, "Looks like you are downsizing."

"What makes you say so?" asked Amit.

"Well, I am called in here and asked to fill in some customer service questionnaire. Such things are done before giving people the pink slip."

Siddharth looked genuinely disturbed. Also, what he had said made sense. *Such things do happen,* thought Amit.

"Don't worry, Siddharth. We are interviewing a few employees. We have to send two employees for a ten-day workshop abroad," said Amit.

"Never heard of such interviews for a paltry ten-day overseas workshop," said Siddharth.

Smart boy, thought Suresh.

"Come on, let's proceed. We heard that you have been to a number of countries," proceeded Amit.

"So?" questioned Siddharth.

"What makes you go abroad often?" continued Amit.

"You can't question me about what I do in my personal life. Please get straight to the point. If you are planning to ask me to quit, please say so. Don't try to camouflage it," said Siddharth, obviously irritated.

"This has nothing to do with throwing you out of the bank. Just tell us who Daniel Brown is," said Amit.

"He is the author of the novel *The Da Vinci Code*."

"And Tom Spark and Mark Smith?"

"Don't know," was Siddharth's response.

"What are the odds in the Chelsea versus Tottenham game to be played tomorrow?" continued Amit.

"Don't know," repeated Siddharth.

"Whom should I wager on—Chelsea or Tottenham?"

"I know nothing about football. Maybe I can help with cricket..."

"So, you are into cricket betting...," accused Amit.

"No, I don't bet, but I am an avid cricket fan. So, I can tell you which team you should bet on."

"So, you have been defrauding the bank to bet on cricket?"

"Did you say defrauding the bank?"

"Yes, defrauding to the tune of Rs 25 lakhs," thundered Amit.

"Tell me what's going on. First, you give me a questionnaire on customer service. Then you tell me you are interviewing me for selection to a ten-day overseas workshop. Now you accuse me of defrauding the bank. Take your time and finally tell me what exactly you are arriving at."

"Some audacity! Giving us time to decide what to ask!" said Suresh.

"Audacity? Why not? When you are insinuating that I have defrauded the bank, what do you expect from me," countered Siddharth. "Sir, please put the cards on the table. Tell me the truth and I shall cooperate. But if you bullshit with me, I shall have to call my lawyer."

Amit was tempted to call the police. Siddharth's choice of words had angered him. Suresh too was agitated, but he preferred to remain quiet. Amit decided to come to the point.

"Siddharth, someone has sent twenty messages over the Interbank Global Messaging system without any underlying transactions."

"And you have concluded it is me," said Siddharth.

"What makes you use the word 'concluded'?" questioned Amit.

"Obviously, you must have investigated deeply into the matter, studied it carefully and found a few suspects, and then pinned me down," replied Siddharth.

Amit was surprised at this reaction. How quickly Siddharth had gauged the situation. Was he the culprit or was he just that sharp to grasp what was untold.

"Siddharth, did you send those messages?" asked Suresh.

"No, I have not sent any such message. And please, I am not a cheat. I can never cheat the institution that provides me my bread and butter. If you can tell me exactly what has happened and your reasons for suspecting me, then maybe I will feel relieved. Right now, I am hating the whole scene," retorted Siddharth.

Amit was impressed by how cleverly and coolly Siddharth had responded. He did not create a scene, display hatred, or look confused or nervous. Amit explained the whole episode to him.

"Okay, I get it, sir. The entries were matched clandestinely. Obviously, someone from the Matching Team has to be the culprit. You must have sifted through the Matching Team and you are now interrogating the suspects," surmised Siddharth.

Amit and Suresh were again impressed by Siddharth's clear logic and thought process.

"Now I feel better. Probably you are justified in suspecting me. But no, I am not the culprit," said Siddharth.

"Siddharth, your grasping of the situation is indeed very good. I am impressed. Who do you think is the culprit then?" asked Amit.

Siddharth asked for some paper and pen and fifteen minutes to analyze everything. While he sat with the pen and paper, the others in the room took the opportunity to make calls and freshen up. Coffee and snacks were served to everyone.

After fifteen minutes or so, Siddharth summarized his suspicions as follows.

Chandrashekhar Rai	Not possible
Nitin Guha	Not possible
Ganesh Thaly	Not possible
Sonam Shah	Not possible
Aditi Manav	Not possible
Narendra Kamath	Possible

"Yes, Narendra Kamath could be the culprit," concluded Siddharth.

"What makes you say that?" asked Amit. He felt uncomfortable. Had they been wrong in roping Narendra to find the culprit? Suresh too feared the same.

"Obviously, the culprit is from the Matching Team. Except Narendra, the team members were allotted the job of matching the entries. Mind you, that was their only objective and target. Narendra was in charge of the team. He reviewed the day's progress. He had a bird's eye view of the entire operations. Also, he was the only one who could sit at any table and not seem out of place. The messaging software was loaded on a couple of computers that were bang opposite Rajesh Naik's cabin, who was the then deputy head of Treasury. None of the Matching Team members could sit at that table without attracting attention. Affirmatively, Narendra is the culprit. At the end of each day, he had a record of all the entries that were pending. Only he could have created such havoc," summarized Siddharth.

Amit and Suresh were stunned. How quickly and logically Siddharth had concluded everything! Was this rehearsed or was it genuine? They asked Siddharth to wait in the Z cubicle along with an official from the Customer Service department.

Amit and Suresh were in a fix. They did not know how to proceed further. They were really concerned. If Narendra indeed was the culprit, was it possible that he had destroyed some records? How would they explain to their bosses their decision to take Narendra on board during the investigation? After debating for long, they finally decided to confront all the members of the Matching Team together. Urgent summons were issued to Narendra Kamath, Nitin Guha, Chandrashekhar Rai and Ganesh Thaly. They were asked to meet Amit at 4 p.m. in the conference hall of the main office.

18

The Joint Confrontation

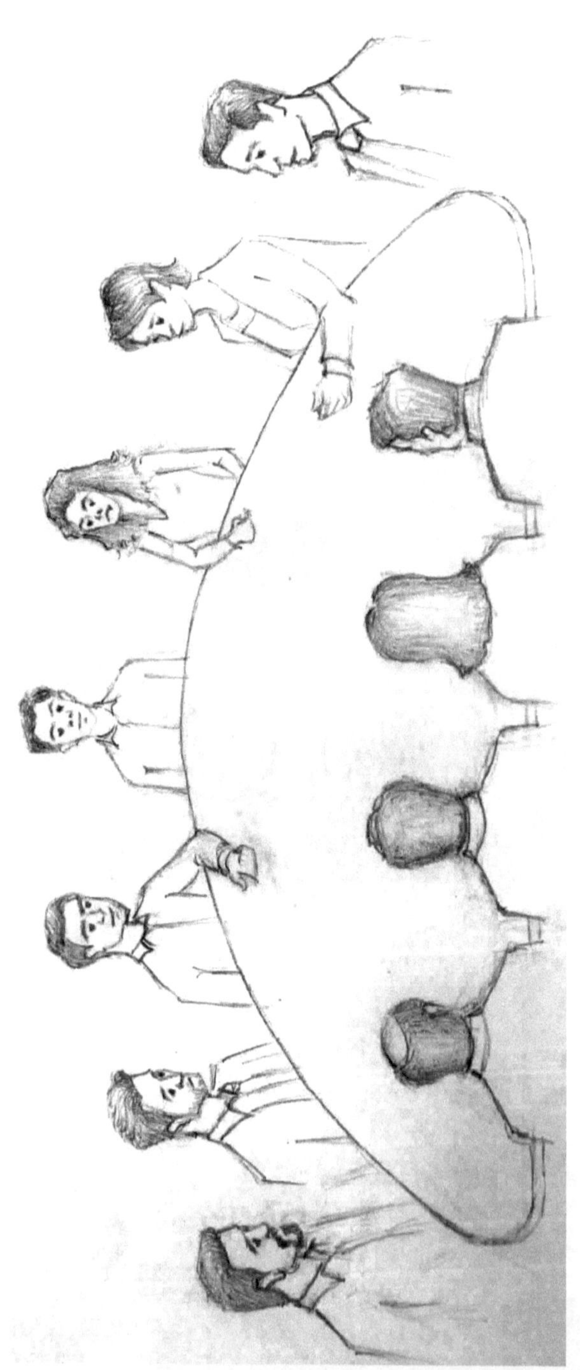

An eerie tension prevailed in the conference hall as Amit Tandon, Suresh Sharma, Dr. Trehan and Ms. Usha Atre sat in a line facing the members of the erstwhile Matching Team, who were seated on chairs placed in a semi-circle. Narendra was seated at the extreme right of the semi-circle. To his right were, Sonam and Aditi. Ganesh sat at the center while Nitin, Chandrashekhar and Siddharth were seated on his right. As was decided earlier, Amit addressed the seven members in a loud and stern voice.

"I request all of you to put your mobiles on silent mode. The circumstances under which we have gathered here are neither pleasant nor desirable. We are looking for a culprit who has defrauded the bank to the tune of Rs 25 lakhs by sending twenty messages over the Interbank Global Messaging system to five accounts in the US without any underlying transaction. We suspect the culprit is one among you. FEMA regulations have been violated. If the culprit owns up, the others will be spared of further ordeal. If not, we will be constrained to lodge an FIR with the police. Then god help all of us. What the police will do is anybody's guess."

Chandrashekhar and Nitin were stunned. Various questions cropped up in their mind.

"This is not possible. Those entries would have remained unmatched and they would have come to our notice," screamed Nitin.

"Absolutely, but that has not happened. The culprit has very cleverly matched all the entries," replied Amit.

"How come all this has come to light after so many years?" asked Chandrashekhar.

"That's immaterial now," replied Amit.

Suresh kept observing everyone. The psychologist too was studying all of them. Aditi's face did not reveal anything. Sonam didn't appear perturbed. She had already gone through this.

"You have already asked me all these questions. Why again?" Sonam asked.

"Quiet," screamed Amit.

"Why me? I have not done anything and you know that," said Ganesh.

"No questions," admonished Amit.

Ganesh was rattled. How had he become a suspect? He looked at Aditi and was tempted to scream, "It's Aditi." Reading his mind, Amit glared at him.

Narendra tried to gauge the situation. Was he really a suspect or was he called as the whole team was being addressed? He cursed himself for not following up with Amit on the progress of the investigation. Siddharth was keenly observing Narendra. It appeared to him as though Narendra was trying to hide his nervousness.

There was pin-drop silence. Tension weighed heavily in the air. Amit decided to wait for fifteen minutes. He closed his eyes and rested his head on the back on his chair. He hated what was going on. He wondered how the day would end. Would he be compelled to lodge an FIR? What would happen then?

Chandrashekhar and Nitin looked at the others.

"Narendra, what's all this?" asked Nitin.

Narendra ignored the question. Nitin turned towards Ganesh and said, "Ganesh, how can they do this to us? Let's ask for lawyers." Sonam joined in. "Yes, yes. We are not cheats. How dare they subject us to such questioning!" she said. Aditi too joined in the protest. Amit chose not to react.

Slowly, tempers started to flare up.

"It's better the culprit owns up now, otherwise all of us will be under suspicion. If the bank files an FIR, then all of us will be treated as culprits and harassed," said Siddharth.

Hearing this, all the others pounced on Siddharth.

"Are you with us or with them?" asked Nitin.

"Listen, there is no us and them. It's only the culprit and the non-culprits. Don't you realize what will happen if the matter goes to the police? All of us will be harassed till the culprit is found," screamed Siddharth.

Now fear gripped everyone. Slowly, the seriousness of the situation started sinking in. Just then, Sonam's mobile phone vibrated. As she picked it up to answer, Amit said, "Please answer only if absolutely necessary." Hearing this, Sonam promptly disconnected the call.

Amit again tried to get a confession. "Look, the culprit is one of you. Sending messages and then clandestinely matching the entries could not have been possible without the involvement of a member from the Matching Team."

"Please tell us the whole story from start to finish," said Chandrashekhar.

"My friend, unfortunately, this is not a story. It's a nightmare that we are all going through. The culprit does not need any details. He or she is very well aware of every minute detail," said Amit.

Again, there was pin-drop silence. Seven pairs of eyes kept shifting from one person to the other. Each one was trying to find the culprit in the group.

Aditi wondered if Siddharth was the culprit. Chandrashekhar was trying to convince himself that this was all a bad dream. Nitin wondered whether one could get drunk on a bottle of Coke, which he had had with his lunch. Sonam wanted to go home; she had an appointment with the dentist at 8 p.m. Narendra's eyes kept shifting from one member to the other. Ganesh's head hammered with just one thought—Aditi is the culprit. Siddharth kept looking at Narendra. An hour later, there was still no confession from anyone.

Amit and Suresh were getting impatient. They discussed the issue for a few minutes after which Amit announced, "The deadline is 7 p.m. If no confession is received by then, we will be compelled to call the police."

Nitin burst out again, "I am calling my lawyer. You can't do this to us."

"Go ahead and call your lawyer. I shall have to lodge the FIR before that, as I have to safeguard the interest of the bank. I have been seeking time from the superiors for the last two months to ensure that only the culprit faces the consequences, or else all of you would have been picked up first and questioned later," snapped Amit.

Narendra observed that Siddharth's glance was repeatedly falling on him. He sensed that Siddharth was suspecting him. He abruptly got up from his seat, walked around listlessly and occupied an empty chair next to Siddharth. Seeing Narendra get up, everyone was stunned. They all thought that Narendra was about to confess. But Narendra looked into Siddharth's eyes and, in a loud and clear voice, said, "Siddharth, I know you are suspecting me. But I am not the culprit. I have neither the caliber nor the motive for such a fraud. Had I been the culprit, I would have left the organization after the act. Mind you, I had and I still do have plenty of offers from other banks and many blue-chip companies." Saying so, he then went back to his original seat.

Suresh and Amit were startled at this. Siddharth too was taken aback. Suddenly, he felt himself freeze. His mind went blank, his heart pounded hard and his palms turned cold. The quick-witted Siddharth was suddenly speechless.

The already tensed atmosphere in the room seemed to stiffen further. Just then, there was a knock on the door and the cafeteria staff walked in with snacks and beverages.

Sonam shouted, "At last something to eat. I am famished. You can serve me first." She looked at the others and suggested, "First eat and then worry."

Amit mentally thanked Sonam for cooling the atmosphere a bit. He said, "Yes, please relax and have your snacks. We shall take a fifteen-minute break."

But no one was in a mood to relax. Everyone quietly finished the snacks and headed to the washrooms, before getting back to the conference room.

The hot coffee refreshed Siddharth and his mind started functioning. Narendra had a valid point. But no one else could have pulled off such a stunt easily, he felt. His mind raced. Did someone who was not present in the room have access to the Matching Software and messaging system?

Meanwhile, the others were busy talking in hushed tones to one another, trying to solve the mystery.

Siddharth decided to discuss his line of thinking with the others.

"Please listen. As per my logic, such a fraud could have been committed only by a person who had a bird's eye view of the unmatched entries and access to the messaging system. Such a person would not have attracted attention."

"Please elaborate," said Chandrashekhar.

"Well, the Matching Team members matched entries the whole day. If I remember correctly, we hardly bothered to look at the unmatched entries. That was looked after by Narendra. Then, to send the Interbank Global Messaging system messages, the culprit would have had to sit at the computer where the messaging software was loaded. This was bang opposite the deputy Treasury head's cabin. None of the Matching Team members could have sat there without attracting attention. So, that rules out the Matching Team members, except Narendra."

"Come on Siddharth, Narendra cannot be the culprit," protested Sonam.

All the others joined her in defending Narendra.

"Wait, wait. Let me finish," pleaded Siddharth. "I am not accusing Narendra. The question is other than Narendra who else could have access to the unmatched entries and messaging system without attracting attention?"

"Again, you are accusing him," said Sonam.

"Narendra, please think in my line of thought. Who else studied the unmatched entries, say on a weekly basis?" asked Siddharth.

"Every week, I had to report the unmatched entries period-wise to the then Treasury head Mehta. But I don't think he was capable of this fraud. Overall, he had an idea of things, but he definitely didn't know the finer nuances," replied Narendra.

"But Octopus poked his arms everywhere, remember?" commented Aditi.

Amit and Suresh were keenly following the conversation.

"Remember how irritating he was? He used to monitor our work unnecessarily," continued Aditi.

"Always wanted to impress Mehta," added Sonam.

"Octopus was Mehta's right-hand man," Chandrashekhar chipped in.

"But that didn't give him the right to monitor us. I did give him a piece of my mind on a couple of occasions," said Sonam.

Narendra's mind went back to those difficult days. Yes, Octopus was indeed Mehta's favorite. But then any boss would have loved to have Octopus as his assistant. He was an efficient, brilliant, hardworking and reliable hand. As Narendra was lost in thoughts, he was brought back to the present by Siddharth's question. "Narendra, Octopus is the culprit. Don't you agree?"

Narendra was dumbfounded. He had been with the investigation team for about two months now. But the possibility of Octopus being the culprit had never occurred to him.

"He left the bank in June 2010," said Ganesh.

The noise levels in the conference room rose a notch. The tension suddenly evaporated. The members of the Matching Team started discussing among themselves animatedly.

Amit and Suresh watched them for another fifteen minutes. Suddenly, things were on a different track.

"Please calm down all of you. Looks like there is a new twist, but please tell us, who is this Octopus," said Amit.

Narendra offered to answer. "He is Vijay Kumar. He was a derivative dealer those days. He was a brilliant man; he was brought in as a dealer by Mehta as they had worked together at the Mumbai forex branch. People said his brain was a mini computer, but many of us believed it was a super computer. His grasping of situations is excellent and he has tremendous stamina to work for long hours. During those turbulent days, he used to stay back after the dealing hours to help Mehta. In fact, he did whatever Mehta asked him to do."

"But why do you call him Octopus?" quipped Suresh.

"I shall answer that sir, as I named him Octopus," said Siddharth. "The octopus is considered the most intelligent among the invertebrates. Vijay is the most intelligent vertebrate I have come across. Also, Vijay's head is bulbous like the octopus. He also has large eyes. An octopus has the ability to blend with the surroundings. You could put Vijay in any place and he would adapt to it so well, as though as he was born and brought up in that very place. Also, an octopus has four pairs of arms. Vijay's arms are capable of handling any amount of work."

"Let us get back to the purpose of gathering here. Do you think Vijay could have committed this fraud?" asked Amit.

"Yes, of course, definitely," shouted all of them in unison.

"Anyone not agreeing?" asked Suresh.

There was no response.

"Can you prove that Vijay Kumar is the culprit?" asked Suresh.

There was quite a din as everyone answered simultaneously.

"How can we prove it?" asked Ganesh.

"Have to think it over," said Nitin.

"Let's find out," offered Chandrashekhar.

"That's not our job," said Sonam.

"We have to prove it, if we have to save ourselves," remarked Siddharth.

Amit was troubled. What could they do now? He had promised his bosses that a final decision would be taken by evening. Now, with a new twist, he would need more time. Observing him, Suresh said that the matter would have to be discussed with the bosses. After a brief discussion with Suresh, Amit addressed the seven members.

"May I have your attention please? Sorry for using the word 'suspect', but the fact is we have one more suspect. Please don't feel offended. But till such time we find some proof against Vijay Kumar, the other ground realities don't change."

Again, there were protests from most of them and now their tone was harsh. Amit had to bang the table to silence all of them.

"How dare you suspect us even now?" shouted Nitin.

"Yes, yes. You can't do anything to us," said Chandrashekhar.

Narendra stood up and addressed them. "Look, what Amit says is correct. Until we gather proof against the culprit, we are all under suspicion. If the bank lodges the FIR, these people won't be able to intervene in the matter. So, let's cooperate."

"Thanks Narendra. I request that we all meet tomorrow for further discussions. Only you people can provide the clues. Ladies, sorry for bothering you on a Sunday, but honestly, I don't have an option. And god help me in convincing my bosses to give us some more time," said Amit.

"Amit, we understand and we shall be here tomorrow. We also appreciate your concern for the innocent. Lodging an FIR was the easiest and safest option for you, but you chose to find the culprit first, thus sparing us the trauma. We are indeed grateful to you and Suresh," said Sonam.

The others too joined Sonam in thanking Amit and Suresh.

"So, we meet here at nine o'clock tomorrow," said Amit.

"Please keep everything confidential. No one should get to know what's going on," said Suresh.

After everyone left, Suresh turned to Dr Trehan, "Do you suspect any one of these to be the culprit?"

"It doesn't seem so. None of them displayed any traits of a fraudster," opined Dr. Trehan.

"Thank you very much, doctor. Please send us your report for our records," said Suresh.

"We have to live with the Damocles sword hanging over us for some more time," rued Amit.

After Dr. Trehan left, Amit and Suresh went to their bosses to apprise them of the outcome of the meeting. Luckily, the bosses were in the main office building after a meeting with a few overseas clients.

It took Amit and Suresh a lot of effort to convince the bosses to grant them some more time before filing the FIR. One of their bosses even went to the extent of insinuating that Amit or Suresh or both of them were involved in the fraud or were being bribed by the culprit. Fortunately, the senior-most boss understood Amit and Suresh's intention and gave them a week's time. He even admonished his junior saying, "You can't subject sincere people to harassment for another person's wrongdoing."

19

Financial Markets and Sports Betting

After reaching home, Amit surfed the internet. He vaguely recollected reading an article earlier 'Many parallels between trading in financial markets and sports betting' by Steven D Levitt. He found it on nber.org. It reads as follows:

First, in both settings, investors with heterogeneous beliefs and information seek to profit through trading as uncertainty is resolved over time.

Second, sports betting, like trading in financial derivatives, is a zero-sum game with one trader on each side of the transaction.

Finally, large amounts of money are potentially at stake.

In the light of these similarities, it is surprising that these two types of markets are organized so differently. In most financial markets, prices change frequently. The prevailing price is that which equilibrates supply and demand.

The primary role of the market makers is to match buyers with sellers. In sports wagering however, market makers (casinos and bookmakers) simply announce a 'price' (which takes the form of a point spread e.g. the home team to win a football game by at least 3.5 points) after which the adjustments are typically small and infrequent. If that price is not the market clearing price, then the bookmakers may be exposed to substantial risk. If bettors are able to recognize and exploit mispricing on the part of the bookmaker, the bookmaker can sustain large losses.

The risk borne by bookmakers on sports betting is categorically different than the casino's risk on other games of chance such as roulette, keno or slot machines. In those games of chance, the odds are stacked in favor of the casinos, and the law of large numbers dictates profits for the house.

In contrast, however, if the bookmaker sets the wrong line on sporting events, it can lose money in the long run. The presence of even a small number of bettors whose skills allow them to achieve positive expected profits could prove financially disastrous to the bookmaker. Such bettors could either amass large bankrolls or, in the presence of credit constraints, sell their information to others.

After reading the article, Amit was tempted to conclude that Vijay Kumar was the culprit. If he was indeed as intelligent as the Matching Team members had claimed him to be, there was every chance that he could outdo the bookmakers.

20

Joint Effort

The next day, Amit, Suresh and the members of the erstwhile Matching Team met at the conference hall of the main office. After greeting one another, all of them sat around the conference table.

Amit started, "Today's agenda is to find proof of Vijay Kumar having committed the fraud. I have listed a few points, which I shall discuss with you all. Thereafter, you can give your inputs.

1. Last night, the HR department confirmed that Vijay Kumar was present on all the days that the messages were sent.
2. His bank accounts were scrutinized. Nothing untoward was found.
3. His personal Assets and Liability statements have also not revealed anything.
4. He resigned from the bank and was relieved on June 30, 2010.

Does anyone know where Vijay Kumar is working now?"

"He joined MNA Bank, worked there for about six months. He is now working with a multinational company," said Ganesh.

"Any idea how we can nail him?" asked Suresh.

"Do what you have done with all of us; call him and confront him," said Chandrashekhar.

"That won't work since he is no longer in our bank," said Amit.

"Just inform the police that Vijay Kumar is the culprit," said Chandrashekar.

"Chandrashekhar, we are not playing a police-and-thief game," said Narendra.

"Let's gather some information about him. Like from which part of the country he is, where he studied and what his life was like earlier," said Aditi.

"Okay Ganesh, probably you can help with that," said Amit.

"I think he is from Himachal Pradesh. Heard he had gone to the US for higher studies. I have never heard anything about his family. We can ask Mehta. He may know more about Vijay," said Ganesh.

"No, no. It may backfire," said Amit. The others too felt the same.

"The HR department must be having all the details regarding his permanent address, his qualifications etc. I shall get all that in an hour's time," said Suresh.

"Meanwhile, please try and recollect anything about Vijay Kumar. Speak up even if it seems irrelevant to you," said Amit.

"Anybody attended any training or conference with him?" asked Suresh.

"I attended a training program with him in Mumbai. His brilliance is so pronounced that one does not notice any other thing about him," said Narendra.

"Does he show off?" asked Suresh.

"No, not at all. He is pretty laidback. Never saw him having ego issues with anyone. In fact, when the other person does not grasp his point of view, he patiently and logically explains it," said Siddharth.

"He had once gone to the US for a conference. I think Anand, the dealer, had accompanied him," said Ganesh.

"We can ask Anand," said Sonam.

Narendra, Suresh and Amit exchanged glances. Fortunately, no one other than them was aware about Anand's suspension. It had been kept highly confidential.

Meanwhile, Suresh received feedback from the HR department.

Vijay Kumar was from a village called Lohna, Palampur, Kangra district in Himachal Pradesh. He graduated in commerce from Government College, Dharamshala. He then did his master's in International Commerce in the US where he worked for a couple of years before returning to India.

The erstwhile members of the Matching Team started discussing Vijay Kumar. They were rather surprised to know that he was from a village. From a village all the way to the US was indeed a long journey. He spoke English just like all of them. His accent did not reveal that he was from a village or that he had stayed in the US for a couple of years. Yes, Octopus was the right nickname for him, they all agreed.

An hour later, everyone concluded that their discussion was leading them nowhere. They had not noticed that both Amit and Suresh were not in the room.

Amit had gone to the adjoining room to talk to Anand about Vijay Kumar's behavior during their trip to the US. During the last fortnight or so, Amit had not taken Anand's calls. Naturally, Anand was upset. "Sir, finally you thought it fit to call me. Do you realize how difficult life has become for me? I am literally under house arrest. No office, can't tell my parents what's going on, I don't go out for fear of bumping into people I know. Sometimes I feel like hanging myself and ending it all."

Amit was taken by surprise at this barrage from Anand. He had been so busy with the office workload and the investigation that Anand's agony had taken a backseat in his mind and memory. He tried to find the right words and tone to calm down Anand. He had to ensure that Anand was not driven down the suicidal lane.

"Anand, please calm down. Think about all those who love and care for you. Like they say, this too will pass."

"Sorry sir, I am really sorry. You are actually trying to help me and I am being outright rude. Do bear with me. Now please tell me the purpose of calling me up."

"Anand, you had gone to the US with Vijay Kumar for a conference. Can you recollect anything unusual about him during your stay there?" asked Amit.

"No, nothing was unusual. In fact, he was the best guide I could have ever had."

"Take your time and get back to me if you recollect anything worth sharing about Vijay Kumar," said Amit.

"Do you think Vijay Kumar is the culprit?" enquired Anand,

"Well, we are going through all the staff members who were on the muster during those days," said Amit.

In the meantime, Suresh had called up a detective agency and asked them to check the background of one Vijay Kumar from Lohana, Palampur, Himachal Pradesh. He shared Vijay Kumar's address and qualifications with the agency.

Then Amit and Suresh joined the others in the conference room. After deliberating for some time, they decided to wind up as the discussions were not proving fruitful. Lunch was served after which the team members left. Narendra was requested to stay back with Amit and Suresh.

21

An Intriguing Revelation

Narendra suggested that Vijay Kumar's computer be checked for leads. But would it be possible to locate the computer used by Vijay Kumar? Even if it was located, would it still have the data stored by him? These were questions hammering Amit's head. As the three of them headed towards Connaught Place, Suresh called Tanmay and asked him to join them at the Treasury department.

Around 4.30 p.m., Amit, Suresh, Narendra and Tanmay were seated in Amit's cabin. As Tanmay had been involved in the initial phase of the investigation, he was not surprised when he was asked to locate Vijay Kumar's computer.

"I hope his computer has not been formatted. Finding the backup would be a little tedious," said Tanmay.

In an hour's time, Tanmay joyfully announced that the computer had been traced and, as luck would have it, the dealer who had replaced Vijay Kumar had been provided with an upgraded computer. So, Vijay Kumar's computer had been disconnected and dumped in the storeroom.

Tanmay searched all the files and folders on the computer for leads. He was asked to search for the names Mark Smith, Tom Spark, Timothy Lopez, Jose Martin and Daniel Brown. Nothing was found. *Only a fool would leave telltale signs,* thought Tanmay.

While Tanmay was busy browsing the computer, there was nothing much Amit, Suresh and Narendra could do. Suresh tried to catch some sleep. Amit utilized the time to make some calls. Narendra busied himself with a crossword puzzle in the newspaper.

As the evening dissolved into night, Tanmay informed the others that he had searched the computer for the given names and the relevant dates with no success. He had also searched for hidden files and hidden data. Most of the files were Excel sheets with day-to-day data of the deals done. The Word files were also related to the daily reporting of profit/loss booked.

"Want me to look for anything else?" asked Tanmay.

"You are the computer expert. I am sure you would have searched for hidden files, hidden drives or whatever," said Amit.

"What about deleted files? Obviously, he would have deleted every bit of information related to the fraud, if he had used this computer for storing his crime records," said Suresh.

"Absolutely no two opinions about that," agreed Amit.

"I don't have the expertise to recover permanently deleted files. I shall check with my friends and batchmates on that," said Tanmay.

As the others were talking, Narendra's eyes fell on the 'UNSCRAMBLE' portion of the newspaper.

"Search for those names spelled backward like Mark Smith as Kram Htims. Then jumble the spelling and search," suggested Narendra.

"Oh yes, that's a great idea," said Tanmay.

About half an hour later, Tanmay announced, "Sorry folks, no luck."

Amit's mind kept asking whether this was a wild goose chase. In that case, they were back to square one.

Narendra offered to have a look at the computer. As he searched, he found a folder named 'Vijay'. On opening it, he found subfolders in which were a number of Excel and Word files. The folders revealed how organized and meticulous Vijay Kumar was. Every morning, he prepared a strategy that was to be adopted for his work. In the evening, he put down the results and gave himself a rating depending on the profit or loss he made.

Narendra gave a live commentary of his observations. "Next, we have many Excel sheets containing the birth dates of family and friends, Bollywood stars, Hollywood stars, politicians, cricketers and footballers. The dates of various matches and so on. Crazy man this Vijay Kumar is! Now we have the telephone numbers of other banks, clients and restaurants. Now what's this? Oh! An Excel sheet of the day-to-day expenses, vegetables, fruits, groceries etc., etc. Here's a subfolder on interesting articles, oil prices, stock market prices, gold prices, global economy, emerging markets..."

Half an hour later, Narendra announced that he would like to copy the folder 'Vijay Kumar' onto his pen drive as it carried a few interesting articles.

Around 9.30 p.m., as everyone was winding up for the day, Suresh received a call on his mobile. He walked out of Amit's cabin to attend the call. His mood lifted as he heard what the caller said. He thanked the caller and promised to get in touch with him the next day.

Amit, Narendra, Suresh and Tanmay walked out of the cabin and took the lift down. After Narendra and Tanmay left, Suresh took Amit's hand and excitedly said, "Congratulations! At last, we are on to something!" Amit thought Suresh was being sarcastic. "Yes, congratulations to all of us. We are back to square one," said Amit.

Suresh was so excited that he missed the sarcasm. "The detective agency called up. They did a background check on Vijay Kumar. They had been to his village at the address given to them by the bank. Guess what?" said Suresh.

Suresh's excitement irritated Amit. He just shook his head and headed towards his car.

"Don't sulk, Amit. We are on to something. There is another Vijay Kumar at the address. He runs a small grocery store and he is a school dropout. On enquiring further, it was learnt that there was another boy by the name Vijay Kumar who was extremely brilliant. Coincidentally, their fathers too had the same name—Krishna Kumar. The brilliant Vijay Kumar got into bad company, which led him to commit petty crimes. When the petty crimes got out of hand, our Vijay Kumar was sent to his uncle's house in a nearby town. Later, this Vijay Kumar did well in studies and went on to Dharamshala for further education. The villagers said that the bright Vijay Kumar had given the address of the other Vijay Kumar in all his documents to avoid being linked to the petty crimes. The good villagers did not object as it didn't affect the other Vijay Kumar in any way."

"Great! Now we can go to the police and tell them Vijay Kumar is the culprit because he has given us the wrong address.

Instead of mentioning house number one, he has mentioned house number two," said Amit sarcastically.

"Amit, cheer up. I understand your frustration. But the fact is Vijay Kumar has a history of petty crimes and he has tried to cover it up. This means there is a possibility of him being the culprit," said Suresh.

"You think this story will convince the higher-ups? What would be my credibility in their eyes after two months?"

"Amit, you can choose to sulk, I can't stop you. But I am positive everything will be sorted out by tomorrow evening. Goodnight."

I don't choose to sulk. My logic says we are back to square one, thought Amit.

The next day was Monday, the start of a new week. Everyone was back at their desks. Narendra had requested Amit for a meeting before office hours, but Amit had a tight schedule. But Suresh was relatively free that day. He called up the detective agency and asked them to find out more about Vijay Kumar.

At 7 p.m., Suresh, Narendra and Tanmay were seated in Amit's cabin.

"Yes Narendra," prompted Amit.

"Tanmay, you will have to boot Vijay Kumar's computer," said Narendra.

Tanmay made arrangements to get the computer from the storeroom. After the computer came alive, Narendra asked Tanmay to open the folder named 'Vijay' and then the file containing birth dates. The file had data on many sheets.

"Go to sheet thirty-nine," said Narendra.

"It's a list of expenses," said Tanmay.

"Now go to row 321 column AL," said Narendra.

Item	Price	Date
Air freshener	25	25/09/08
Apple	72	05/12/08
Hair oil	46	25/09/08
Ice tray	106	05/12/08
Ink	43	25/09/08
Kitchen scrub	29	25/09/08
Knife	90	05/12/08
Maggi	42	25/09/08
Maize	23	25/09/08
Melon	180	05/12/08
Mushroom	59	05/12/08
Oats	56	05/12/08
Paper	67	05/12/08
Raisins	26	25/09/08
Rose syrup	87	05/12/08
Shoe polish	40	25/09/08
Soap	65	05/12/08
Tamarind	98	05/12/08
Toothpick	54	05/12/08
Toothpaste	45	25/09/08

"Looks like some supermarket bill," said Tanmay.

"Now, sort it in ascending order of the price," requested Narendra.

Item	Price	Date
Maize	23	25/09/08
Air freshener	25	25/09/08
Raisins	26	25/09/08
Kitchen scrub	29	25/09/08
Shoe polish	40	25/09/08
Maggi	42	25/09/08
Ink	43	25/09/08
Toothpaste	45	25/09/08
Hair oil	46	25/09/08
Toothpick	54	05/12/08
Oats	56	05/12/08
Mushroom	59	05/12/08
Soap	65	05/12/08
Paper	67	05/12/08
Apple	72	05/12/08
Rose syrup	87	05/12/08
Knife	90	05/12/08
Tamarind	98	05/12/08
Ice tray	106	05/12/08
Melon	180	05/12/08

"It's the same bill in a different order," said Tanmay.

"Look at it from our point of view," said Narendra.

Amit, Suresh and Tanmay looked at the screen and tried to make some sense of it. Almost simultaneously they thumped the table.

"Yes! I got it," said Amit.

"Brilliant, Narendra," exclaimed Tanmay.

"Great job, Narendra, truly brilliant. But how did you find it?" asked Suresh.

"Last evening, here in office, when I was going through this folder, this particular Excel file stuck out like a sore thumb. Why would anyone note down so many birth dates, those of film stars, politicians, sports persons and all? That's the reason I copied the folder onto my pen drive. I went through each and every sheet trying to find some clue. I found data like names of countries, cities, movies and so on. I was convinced it was a camouflage. I must have gone through all the fifty-eight Excel sheets at least twenty times each. I sorted the data on each sheet in every possible way.

As a last straw, I decided to go from top to bottom and left to right of each and every sheet. I found nothing till sheet thirty-eight. While doing this exercise on sheet thirty-nine, I found the treasure. At first glance, it appeared to be an ordinary bill. Then, as I sorted the table in the ascending order of price, my eyes scrolled down the list. I read the first letter of every item, Mark Smith and Tom Spark popped out.

Sheet thirty-nine has data from rows 1 to 121 and columns A to J. Rows 122 to 320 and columns K to AK are blank. That's the reason I missed our treasure earlier, while studying the sheet. Probably, a blessing that this data was separate. Otherwise, it would have got jumbled with the other data while sorting and the name of the beneficiaries would not have popped up," said Narendra.

Item	Price	Date
Maize	23	25/09/08
Air freshener	25	25/09/08
Raisins	26	25/09/08
Kitchen scrub	29	25/09/08
Shoe polish	40	25/09/08
Maggi	42	25/09/08
Ink	43	25/09/08
Toothpaste	45	25/09/08
Hair oil	46	25/09/08
Toothpick	54	05/12/08
Oats	56	05/12/08
Mushroom	59	05/12/08
Soap	65	05/12/08
Paper	67	05/12/08
Apple	72	05/12/08
Rose syrup	87	05/12/08
Knife	90	05/12/08
Tamarind	98	05/12/08
Ice tray	106	05/12/08
Melon	180	05/12/08

"At what time, did you stumble upon this, Narendra?" asked Suresh.

"Around 3.30 a.m.," replied Narendra.

"I can understand your anxiety. You were the next probable suspect," said Suresh.

"Are there any more such sheets?" asked Tanmay.

"No. I went through all the sheets in the entire folder. It appears that Vijay Kumar deleted all the data related to the fraud. But as they say, every criminal leaves behind some trail, our criminal too goofed up," said Narendra.

"Deleting the entire folder would have been the most natural choice for him. I was surprised yesterday on learning that he had not deleted his files," observed Suresh.

"Was it oversight or was it overconfidence?" questioned Tanmay.

"Whatever is the reason, we are lucky he left a trail and Narendra actually stumbled upon it," said Suresh.

"Tanmay, could you find out about the recovery of permanently deleted/lost files?" asked Amit.

"Yes, a friend who has vast experience in such recovery has promised to come over and help recover the deleted files if possible," said Tanmay.

The next day on Tuesday, around noon, an FIR was lodged with the Economic Offences Wing of the local police and Vijay Kumar was arrested. To everyone's surprise, Vijay Kumar did not resist the arrest. In fact, he did not even ask for bail. His friends and colleagues secured his release on bail.

Wednesday saw a relieved and relaxed Amit back at his desk. His only worry was Anand's future.

A week later, Anand was asked to submit his resignation for his misdeed of quoting four decimal rates to AEL in violation of the bank's guidelines. Amit was able to convince the management that this punishment would suffice, keeping in view the mental torture faced by Anand in the last couple of months for the deeds of Vijay Kumar being attributed to him.

Lalit was commended for his alertness and sharp response that helped unearth the fraud.

22

The Manipulator's Mindset

Months later, Amit happened to meet Vijay Kumar, who was out on bail, at a restaurant. His only question to Vijay Kumar was, "What made you do this?"

Vijay Kumar stared at Amit for a few minutes. He then closed his eyes and answered, "What made me send those messages through the Interbank Global Messaging system? This question has haunted me for the last couple of months. Do you know that the company I work for has not sacked me even after the FIR filed by you? Sacking me or asking for my resignation should have obviously followed my arrest. But the CEO of the company preferred to send me to a counselor."

Saying this, Vijay Kumar started laughing. He then said, "Probably the CEO himself needs counseling is the opinion of many in the company."

"What did the counselor say?" asked Amit.

Vijay Kumar was pensive and did not answer.

Amit let a few minutes pass before he repeated his question.

"What made you do it?"

After a long bout of silence, Vijay Kumar answered, "My extraordinarily brilliant brain. A brilliant brain needs proper guidance and proper channeling. As it grasps things very quickly, it has ample spare time. It demands new challenges every day. Mundane daily routines are too boring for the mind. Control of mind should have been taught to me in early childhood."

"Let's talk about your life," Amit nudged him further.

"Past or future? What's the use of talking about the past? And who knows the future?"

"You sure sound philosophical but again what made you do it?"

"Like I said, my brilliant brain. A child with an extraordinary brain is born in a small village where the only thing the villagers know is farming. The child is sent to a small village school, which has only one teacher. The teacher recognizes and appreciates the child's ability to learn fast but does not understand why he is naughty and restless. As the child grows, so does the list of complaints against his mischiefs. No one understands the torture the child undergoes when his supersonic brain is placed in a class of ordinary children. Later, the child is sent to his uncle's house in a nearby town. There too, no one knows how to handle him. The child then meets a *swami* who reads his mind and tries to calm it by teaching him meditation, but the people of the town drive away the *swami*, mistaking him to be a kidnapper. The child grows into a young lad, completes his education and moves to bigger cities where he sees ample opportunities for his brain."

Vijay Kumar closed his eyes and fell silent. Amit waited for him to continue but it appeared that he had dosed off. Amit gently shook Vijay Kumar's arm and asked, "Then what happened?"

"Some other time, brother," replied Vijay Kumar, starting to get up.

"No no. Don't leave it midway," protested Amit.

"Any particular reason why I should oblige you?" asked Vijay Kumar.

"No, of course not."

"So, goodbye Mr..., whatever your name is," said Vijay Kumar and walked out of the restaurant.

Amit sat back on his chair trying to analyze his own feelings. Vijay Kumar's abrupt departure left him confused. He called the waiter, settled his bill and walked towards his parked car. He wondered whether Vijay Kumar had deliberately left his narrative midway or whether he was short of time. Amit leaned against his car and closed his eyes. He felt annoyed with Vijay Kumar. After a couple of minutes, Amit decided to forget the conversation and move on to his next task. Just as he unlocked the car, he felt a tap on his shoulder.

"Hey brother, hold on."

Recognizing Vijay Kumar's voice, Amit turned around.

"I have changed my mind. Let's sit somewhere, I shall continue my story," said Vijay Kumar.

"Some other time, big brother," replied Amit.

"Looks like I have annoyed you."

"That doesn't matter. Who knows, you may once again decide to stop the conversation midway and walk out. So, let's say good bye," countered Amit.

"You are right, brother. Let's sit on that bench over there," said Vijay Kumar as he moved towards a bench in the adjoining park. Reluctantly, Amit followed him.

"What made you change your mind?" asked Amit.

"You. After walking out of the restaurant, I felt your concern was genuine. Not that it matters, but anyway let's complete the story."

The lights in the park started to turn on as dusk descended on the city.

"The city of Delhi threw up plenty of opportunities for my brain. There was computer programming, research, science and technology."

"But I thought you had studied commerce," said Amit.

"Yes, but my brain grasped science very easily. I could write complicated programs faster than the computer engineers. But alas there was no thrill," said Vijay Kumar.

Amit's facial expression conveyed his surprise.

"Have you ever tried to write a program? Most boring. You know where you are and you know what you want. All you have to do is find a way out. No surprises, no uncertainty, no adrenaline flowing. Only boredom," said Vijay Kumar.

Again, Vijay Kumar closed his eyes and fell silent. This time Amit decided to just watch him and not prompt him.

After a couple of minutes, Vijay Kumar continued, "Again no change. I was bored. Friends were going to the US to study. I too joined the bandwagon. I had heard so much about the land of opportunities. I secured admission for a master's program in International Commerce in Washington. Life was good. I earned my maintenance money by helping students with their assignments.

One of the few plus points of a brilliant brain is everyone wants to be on your friends list."

"Few plus points? I think there are plenty," blurted Amit.

"Like what?" asked Vijay Kumar.

"Well, for a brain like yours, academics is a cakewalk. No hard work required, no burning the midnight oil. Entrance exams are a breeze, university admissions are easy. Job opportunities are aplenty, and the icing on the cake is you have plenty of spare time," said Amit.

"But where's the excitement? There is only boredom. And what does one do with plenty of time at hand? There are no challenges and no one to compete with. It's like having to live with primary school children all the time."

Vijay Kumar's perspective startled Amit.

"But one should diversify one's interests. Sports, athletics, music and theater are some of the options available. You can't complain," protested Amit.

"No no. You don't understand. My brain looks for intellectual adrenaline rush. It's not wired like ordinary brains to look for gratification elsewhere."

"Okay please carry on," said Amit, reminding himself that he was here to listen to Vijay Kumar and not advise him.

"Then one day I was introduced to Mark Smith who was a college level football player. On weekends, some of us from the university went to watch him play. Mingling with football lovers was like living in another world. One day, I heard them discussing sports betting. The concept excited me. Initially, I just hung around them and listened to their jargon. Punter, bookie, bookmaker, odds, win bets, total bets, etc., etc. Mastering the theory part was no big deal. Winning bets was the tricky and exciting part and it sure required a lot of study."

"Initially, I bet small amounts. After losing a few hundred dollars, I succeeded in convincing myself to withdraw from betting. But then it's depressing to withdraw after having lost. The mind tricks you into trying just one more time. Then you repeat your 'last' try, till you win the bet. Then after winning the so-called last bet, you are drawn into a whirlpool of addiction. But I didn't get addicted; I just got attracted to the process of bookmaking. But by then, I was required to return to India after the completion of my studies, as my father was seriously ill. Later, I joined ZNI Bank. After a couple of months, the job became routine and my brain started scouting for challenges. Again, I got attracted to sports betting—not as a punter but as a bookmaker. I studied the scene from a bookie's lens. That's where the adrenaline flows faster. Wow! With so many variables, it sure is exciting."

Vijay Kumar again fell silent.

Amit was now hooked. Though the subject of betting had never caught his fancy, Vijay Kumar's exciting narrative showed him a different world.

"For what purpose was the messaging money used?" asked Amit.

"To get insider information from the bookmaker. Not to win bets, but to study the bookie's technique. I think I have mastered it," answered Vijay Kumar.

"But you could have used your own money. Why risk your career? Or did you think you would never get caught?" asked Amit.

"Me getting caught is a byproduct of some other fraud. I don't know the exact details of this other fraud, but it's by fluke you caught me."

"You don't sound regretful."

"No regrets either for the fraud or for getting caught," said Vijay Kumar.

"You mean to say you have done no wrong?" asked Amit, irritated.

"No," said Vijay Kumar nonchalantly.

Amit looked at him, his eyes searching for an explanation.

"You so-called honest, sincere and dedicated people have a tilted sense of morality. What do you do when you go selling your bank products to clients? You camouflage the products to present them as the best in the industry. You don't lie directly, but you present a rosy picture with a distorted mirror. While quoting rates, you quote the worst rates to the small and gullible clients, but to corporates you quote attractive rates to grab business," argued Vijay Kumar.

"But that's how the system works," protested Amit.

"According to you, if everyone is cheating it's okay. Then that is not labeled cheating. It's called system functioning," countered Vijay Kumar.

"But that's how we book profits. We are not a charitable, not-for-profit organization."

"Everything is right as long as it rakes in profits," said Vijay Kumar sarcastically.

"Vijay Kumar, don't mix issues. You have actually robbed the bank. Do you realize what would have happened if we had not succeeded in nailing you? Innocent people would have been harassed needlessly."

"Do you realize what happens when the so-called star performers of an organization achieve their targets? Yes, they are promoted, given better salaries and perks. What happens to the non-performers? They are looked down upon, denied promotion and sometimes asked to quit. Is that fair? Maybe the non-performer worked much more than the performer, but his conscience didn't permit him to camouflage the product details. Or perhaps he did not have much clout in the organization. So, the company sacks him. But that's okay as per corporate practices. So, you certify it as 'correct'. Under the garb of survival of the fittest, is it okay to kill the weak?" argued Vijay Kumar.

"Vijay Kumar, I don't understand your reasoning. Maybe we can talk about this some other time. I have an appointment in half an hour."

"Yes, we should talk. I can lay bare the so-called moral values of organizations."

Amit got up to take leave. Not knowing whether he would meet Vijay Kumar again, he decided to speak his mind.

"I think I have ruined your future by nailing you. After today's discussion, I am not sure whether it is good or bad for you. Such a bright brain would be wasted if sent to prison. And I am afraid, the company of criminals may swing you to the negative extreme. Your brain may find an adrenaline rush planning an escape from prison."

"On the contrary, I think you have done me a favor. The prison will definitely limit my options. As you guessed, escaping from prison does appeal to me. But no, I have made up my mind to move towards spirituality. That's another kind of high. And it is in the right direction," said Vijay Kumar, as they walked out of the park.

"That's great. But do ensure that the mystic powers once acquired are not employed for the wrong purposes," said Amit, as he turned towards his car.

Both of them laughed and parted ways.